math

for Christian Schools® 4

Bob Jones University Press
Greenville, South Carolina 29614

Marilyn Elmer, B.S., M.S., Education

Ruth Dennison, B.A., Mathematics
Larry Dean Lemon, B.A., M.S., Mathematics
Robert R. Taylor, B.S., M.A., Ph.D., Mathematics

Designed by
Joyce Keller and Jim McGinness

Graphics coordinated by
Joyce Landis

Illustrated by

Linda Eller	Kathy Pflug
Jim Hargis	Ron Seifert
Joyce Landis	Jim Thomas
Jim McGinness	Del Thompson

Math for Christian Schools® : Book 4

Produced in cooperation with the Bob Jones University Department of Mathemathics of the College of Arts and Science, the School of Education, and Bob Jones Elementary School.

ISBN 0-89084-084-9
© 1980 Bob Jones University Press
Greenville, South Carolina 29614

Contents

Unit 1

The Hinckley Fire

The summer of 1894 was dry. Eastern Minnesota had not had rain since April; so no one was surprised when a small forest fire broke out south of the village of Hinckley. People were surprised at how fast it grew. On August 30 the smoke from the fire hung lightly over Hinckley. Yet two days later, the smoke was so thick that the people could not even see the sun. When the sun did reappear, nearly 500 people were dead from the great Hinckley fire.

On the day of the fire the railroads that ran through Hinckley transported all the people who wanted to leave. Hundreds of people escaped on the trains, but many could not bear to leave their homes and businesses. They refused to believe that the fire would really burn the town. They refused to leave even when many buildings were on fire and the last train whistled for them.

That last train left only when the railroad ties started to burn under it. Rather than risk the worst of the fire, the engineer ran the train backwards as fast as he could. Twice he fainted because of the thick smoke. The fire was so hot that the glass in the engine's window shattered. The great engine's throttle was so hot that the engineer's hands were badly burned. Still he kept on. He ran across burning bridges, and then even the train itself started to burn. Still he kept on. Finally, he brought the train to safety. Yet Aylmer Gray, this heroic engineer, would never be completely satisfied with his escape from the fire. He had not been able to help the 500 people who wouldn't leave.

Many people today are no wiser than those people in Hinckley nearly 100 years ago. They know that they are in need of salvation. They may even know all about God's free offer, but they ignore it. They hold on to what they have and refuse to believe that they will ever die. God waits for them to accept His gift, but finally there is no more time, and they are eternally lost. (See II Corinthians 6:2.)

Goals for Unit 1

1. I will try to understand why we study mathematics.
2. I will learn how our number system works.
3. I will be able to round numbers to the nearest ten or hundred.
4. I will understand the addition operation.
5. I will understand the subtraction operation.
6. I will know all the addition and subtraction facts.
7. I will be able to add and subtract when renaming is necessary.
8. I will know the order principle and the grouping principle for addition.

Words to Remember

Hindu-Arabic
digits
ones' place
tens' place
hundreds' place
round
addition
subtraction
"take-away"

"comparing"
"finding the missing addend"
"finding the unknown part"
fact team
order principle
grouping principle
zero principle
rename

What do you remember?

1. Write the standard form of these numbers.
   a. 400 + 50 + 8
   b. 500 + 2
   c. 1,000 + 300 + 40
   d. 10,000 + 2,000 + 100
   e. 4,000 + 40
   f. 300 + 2

2. Write the least number you can, using these digits.
   a. 6, 9, 3
   b. 5, 1, 2
   c. 9, 8, 7

3. Write the greatest number you can, using these digits.
   a. 4, 8, 2
   b. 1, 0, 7
   c. 5, 9, 2

4. Write a numeral with
   a. 7 in the thousands' place.
   b. 0 in the hundreds' place.
   c. 5 in the ten-thousands' place.

5. Write two addition facts and two subtraction facts using these three numbers: 8, 17, 9.

6. Copy and complete. Use the signs $>$, $<$, or $=$.
   a. 300 + 50 + 6 $\square$ 366
   b. 900 + 80 + 3 $\square$ 893
   c. 500 + 160 + 7 $\square$ 676
   d. 900 + 100 + 10 $\square$ 1,000

7. Solve.

a.	**b.**	**c.**
8	16	89
3	27	27
+ 7	+ 58	+ 58

8. Solve.

a.	**b.**	**c.**
88	67	72
- 53	- 27	- 18

9. Write an equation for each problem. Solve.
   a. Maxine had thirty-five cents. She received fifty-five cents for taking two dogs for a walk. How much money does she have now?
   b. Todd needs sixty-five dollars for a bike. He has saved twenty-nine dollars from mowing lawns for eight weeks. How much more money does he need?

Why do we have
to study math?

Have you ever asked the
question Tommy is asking? Do
you think it is really necessary
to study math? Let's find out!

Make a list of times you have
used mathematics this week.

This is part of Tommy's list.
Does your list include some of
these same things?

1. knew when to get up
2. knew when to leave for school
3. counted out money for lunch
4. kept score in a game at recess
5. kept track of time I practiced piano
6. counted plates, glasses, and silverware
   when I set the table
7. found the chapter and verse during devotions
8. bought a dozen eggs, a gallon of milk,
   and a pound of meat for Mom

We study mathematics because we use it every day.
Children use it and adults use it. Ask your parents how
they use math in their work.

Mathematics helps us learn about God

Did you know that mathematics can help you learn more about God? Most of the things we know about God we learn from the Bible. He is Holy. He knows all things. He can do whatever He wills to do. He is everywhere. But Psalm 19:1 says, "The heavens declare the glory of God; and the firmament sheweth His handywork."

This is where math helps us. Scientists must use math to build the telescopes and other instruments they need to learn about space. With math they can predict many years ahead exactly when and where an eclipse of the sun or moon will occur. They can know where certain stars will be in the heavens. Scientists can do these things because the planets, the stars, and other heavenly bodies move through space in an orderly way. We know from this that our God, Who created the heavens, is a God of order.

Scientists have found through searching the heavens that the number of stars is so great that our minds cannot even imagine it. The Bible says that God knows all the stars and calls them by name. If you counted one star each second for your whole life without stopping, you could count only about two billion stars. Yet there are many more than that. Mathematics helps us to know something of how great our God is.

When we look at the earth that God has
made, we see flowers, trees, birds, and insects
with many beautiful colors and patterns. We can
learn from this that God loves beauty. We can also
see that God created many designs when He made the
world. When you study designs, you are studying a kind
of mathematics called *geometry*. The French mathemati-
cian Pascal was so impressed by the geometric designs
he saw in creation that he said, "God is the great
Geometer."

See how many geometric designs you find in the pictures.

Here are more examples of order and pattern in the world that God has created.

Cut an apple into two parts from side to side. What design do you see? Does the apple have a design about the same as this one?

These are salt crystals that have been magnified 25 times. What shape are they? When salt turns into crystals, it always makes this shape.

Butterflies and moths look much alike, but these pictures show one way they are different. Moths have feathery antennas. Butterflies never do. God designed these insects this way.

Our number system is sometimes called the **Hindu-Arabic** number system. It was invented by the Hindus about two thousand years ago. They were a group of people who lived in Asia. The Arabs learned about this way of writing numbers about 700 years later, and they took it into Europe. It was not until about the time of Columbus that the use of written forms of addition, subtraction, multiplication, and division became common. Before that, figuring was done on an abacus or on fingers. Some people think that our number system is one of the world's greatest inventions. God gave men the intelligence to invent our number system. He has given us the intelligence to learn how this system works so that we can use it properly.

Our number system is based on *ten.* It needs only ten **digits**–0, 1, 2, 3, 4, 5, 6, 7, 8, and 9–to represent a number no matter how great the number is. Can you imagine how hard it would be to learn to read and write numbers if we had fifty or a hundred digits to remember instead of only ten?

Our number system has *place value.* Examine these numbers.

13 (3 means 3 ones)   32 (3 means 3 tens)
346 (3 means 3 hundreds)

The 3 has a different *value* in each one because it is in a different *place* in each one.

Three-digit numerals

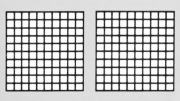

2 hundreds   4 tens   3 ones

hundreds	tens	ones
2	4	3

200 + 40 + 3   243

Expanded form   Standard form

Table form

1. Write the following in expanded form.

hundreds	tens	ones
5	3	2

hundreds	tens	ones
2	4	8

2. Write the following in standard form.
   a. 600 + 30 + 4   c. 900 + 40 + 3
   b. 500 + 20 + 7   d. 600 + 5

3. Write the following in standard form.
   a. six hundred thirty   c. nine hundred ten
   b. five hundred forty-two   d. eight hundred six

4. Tell what the 7 in each numeral means.
   a. 374   b. 782   c. 157   d. 437   e. 765

5. Write the following in standard form.
   a. 6 tens   b. 5 ones   c. 8 hundreds
      2 ones   2 hundreds   0 ones
      4 hundreds   0 tens   6 tens

6. What is the greatest three-digit numeral?

Four-digit numerals

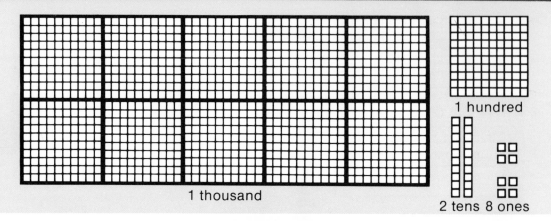

1 hundred

2 tens 8 ones

1 thousand

thousands	hundreds	tens	ones
1	1	2	8

Table form

1,000 + 100 + 20 + 8
Expanded form

1,128
Standard form

1. Write the following in standard form.

   a. 5,000 + 200 + 60 + 3   **d.** 7,000 + 200 + 90 + 6

   b. 8,000 + 600 + 20 + 6   **e.** 1,000 + 800 + 70

   c. 2,000 + 600 + 8   **f.** 6,000 + 500

2. Write the following in expanded form.

   a. 3,926   **b.** 4,872   **c.** 5,930   **d.** 8,437

3. Write the next three numerals. (Example: 1,995; 1,996; 1,997; 1,998)

   a. 1,108   **b.** 2,439   **c.** 2,098   **d.** 4,599   **e.** 4,997

4. Write the numeral that is 10 greater than

   a. 564
   b. 3,405
   c. 6,492
   d. 29
   e. 195

5. Write the numeral that is 100 greater than

   a. 348
   b. 952
   c. 86
   d. 3,484
   e. 8,999

6. Write the numeral that is 1,000 greater than

   a. 4,622
   b. 214
   c. 36
   d. 100
   e. 6,241

You know that when you write a numeral, it is important to put each digit in its proper *place*. The number four hundred sixty-two is written by putting a 4 in the **hundreds' place,** a 6 in the **tens' place,** and a 2 in the **ones' place.**

hundreds	tens	ones
4	6	2

Examine this chart.

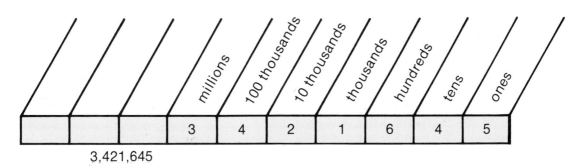

3,421,645

1. What is the value of the place farthest to the right?
2. Notice the value of each place going from right to left.
   a. How many ones equal one ten?
   b. How many tens equal one hundred?
   c. How many hundreds equal one thousand?
   d. How many thousands equal one ten-thousand?
   e. How many ten-thousands equal one hundred-thousand?
   f. How many hundred-thousands equal one million?
3. What do you think will be the value of the next two places at the left of the chart?
4. 1,000,000,000 This number is read "one billion." How many zeroes are there? The place farthest to the left in this chart is the *billions'* place.

What does the 1 mean?

millions	100 thousands	10 thousands	thousands	hundreds	tens	ones	
		2	5	1	6	2	25,162
	1	4	6	8	2	4	146,824
1	0	0	0	0	0	0	1,000,000
		1	7	0	6	2	17,062
8	4	5	1	6	5	4	8,451,654

1. Tell what the 3 means in each numeral.
   a. 23,162   **b.** 3,452,156   **c.** 231,147   **d.** 8,372,100   **e.** 16,314

2. Write a numeral that has
   a. a 5 in the thousands' place.
   b. an 8 in the millions' place.
   c. a 0 in the hundred-thousands' place.
   d. a 6 in the hundreds' place.
   e. a 7 in the ten-thousands' place.

3. Write the following in standard form.
   a. six million
   b. twenty-five thousand, fifty-six
   c. four hundred forty-eight thousand
   d. fifty-eight thousand, two hundred twenty
   e. seven million, two hundred-thousand

4. Complete the tables.

Digits	Greatest number	Least number
6,3,4,8		
1,3,9,2,6		
5,3,1,9		
7,1,8,6,3		
1,4,8,5		

Digits	Greatest number	Least number
3,7,5,2,4		
9,1,1,2,1		
3,7,9,9		
8,5,3,7,4		
3,6,4,4,3		

Comparing numbers

1. Look in the Bible to find how long each of these men
   lived. List their names and ages. (A score is twenty.)

Noah	Genesis 9:29
Abraham	Genesis 25:7
Isaac	Genesis 35:28
Jacob	Genesis 47:28
Joseph	Genesis 50:26
Moses	Deuteronomy 34:7
Joshua	Joshua 24:29
David	II Samuel 5:4

2. Write a number sentence that compares the ages of these men. Use
   >,<, or =. (Remember > means *is greater than;* < means *is less
   than.*)

   a. Noah   Moses

   b. David   Joseph

   c. Moses   Isaac

   d. Joshua   Joseph

   e. Abraham   Jacob

   f. David   Moses

3. Compare these numbers. Use >,<, or =.
   a. 1,346 □ 1,364
   b. 2,300 □ 3,200
   c. 36,130 □ 26,129
   d. 7,103 □ 7,301
   e. 7,295 □ 5,927
   f. 10,000 □ 9,999
   g. 6,359 □ 6,539
   h. 55,505 □ 55,055

4. Write the numeral that is
   a. 100 more than 5,624
   b. 10 less than 355
   c. 1,000 less than 10,654
   d. 100 more than 927
   e. 1 more than 9,999
   f. 1,000 more than 136
   g. 100 less than 1,000
   h. 10 less than 605
   i. 10 more than 1,999
   j. 1,000 less than 20,000

There are 53 books in Miss Allison's classroom. How many is that to the nearest ten?

Is 53 closer to 50 or 60?
There are 50 books to the nearest ten.

1. Examine these examples.

89 **rounded** to the nearest ten is 90.

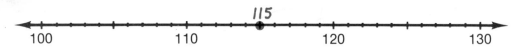

115 **rounded** to the nearest ten is 120.
(When a number is in the middle, round up.)

2. Round these numbers to the nearest ten.

a. 48	**e.** 119	**i.** 92
b. 63	**f.** 154	**j.** 185
c. 95	**g.** 205	**k.** 39
d. 82	**h.** 238	**l.** 264

Rounding numbers to the nearest hundred

There are 2,643 books in the library at Eastside Christian
School. How many is that to the nearest hundred?

2,643

| 2,600 | 2,700 | 2,800 |

Is it closer to 2,600 or 2,700?

1. Examine these examples.

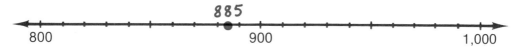

885

| 800 | 900 | 1,000 |

885 rounded to the nearest hundred is 900.

1,450

| 1,400 | 1,500 | 1,600 |

1,450 rounded to the nearest hundred is 1,500.

2. Round these numbers to the nearest hundred.

a. 284	**e.** 1,624	**i.** 1,037
b. 675	**f.** 1,982	**j.** 429
c. 915	**g.** 2,653	**k.** 16,741
d. 350	**h.** 1,850	**l.** 2,350

One of the most important reasons we study mathematics is that we need it to solve problems that we have in our lives every day. We must learn *how* to add, subtract, multiply, and divide, and we must also learn *when* to use these operations to solve problems. We will review **addition** and **subtraction** now. Later we will review multiplication and division.

Addition

Jane has five balls.   Jim has three balls.

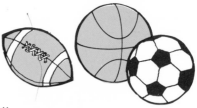

Eric has six balls.

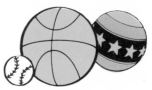

How many balls do they have in all?

5 + 3 + 6 = 14

addends   sum

This is an *addition equation.* It tells us that when a set of five, a set of three, and a set of six are joined together, a set of fourteen is made.

1. Tell in your own words when we use the addition operation.

2. Write a story problem for each of these addition equations. Find the answers.

    a. 63 + 24 = ____   **c.** 30 + 12 + 17 = ____
    b. $1.25 + $0.63 = ____   **d.** $2.10 + $0.57 = ____

Subtraction

We use the subtraction operation in at least three different situations.

"Take-away" subtraction

Nine boxcars were waiting in the yard. The switching engine came and took three of them away. How many boxcars were left?

$$9 - 3 = 6$$
minuend   subtrahend   difference

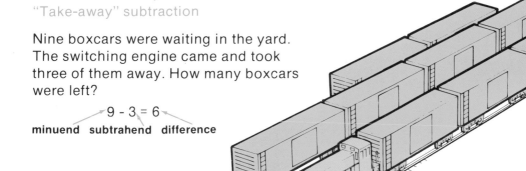

We write a subtraction equation to show that when a set of three is taken from a set of nine, a set of six is left.

1. Tell in your own words when we use the "take-away" subtraction operation.
2. Write a "take-away" subtraction story problem for each of these equations. Find the answers.

   a. 36 - 12 = ___   **b.** 18 - 15 = ___   **c.** 75¢ - 20¢ = ___

3. Write a subtraction equation for each of these pictures. How many are left?

a.

b.

Subtraction

"Comparing" subtraction

Jill has ten books. Tina has seven books. Jill has how many more books than Tina?

    10 - 7 = ____

We write a "comparing" subtraction equation to show that when a set of ten is compared to a set of seven, there are three more in the set of ten than there are in the set of seven. (It also tells us that the set of seven has three less in it than the set of ten.)

1. Tell in your own words when we use the "comparing" subtraction equation.

2. Write a "comparing" subtraction story problem for each of these equations. Find the answers.

    a. 25 - 8 = ___   **b.** 74 - 36 = ___   **c.** $0.90 - $0.70 = ___

3. Write a subtraction equation for each of these pictures. How many more are there?

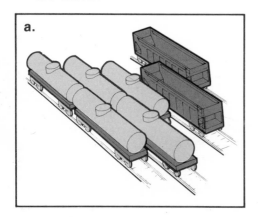

18

Subtraction

"Finding-the-missing-addend" subtraction

Bob wants to buy a candy bar that costs
18¢. He has 12¢. How many more cents
does he need?

$$18¢ - 12¢ = \underline{\qquad}$$

We write a subtraction sentence to find
out that six cents must be added to the
twelve cents to make eighteen cents.

1. Tell in your own words when we use the "finding-the-
   missing-addend" subtraction operation.

2. Write a "finding-a-missing-addend" subtraction story
   problem for each of these equations. Find the
   answers.

   a. $25 - 12 = \underline{\quad}$ **b.** $50 - 15 = \underline{\qquad}$ **c.** $\$0.92 - \$0.82 = \underline{\quad}$

3. Write a subtraction equation for each of these pictures. How many more
   are needed?

   a.

   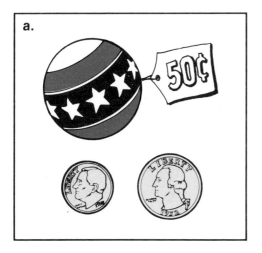

   b.

"Finding-an-unknown-part" subtraction

There are eighteen students in Mrs. Mack's class. Ten of these students are girls. How many boys are in the class?

Girls   Boys

18 - 10 =

We can write a subtraction equation to show that a set of eighteen has been separated into two parts. Since one part has ten in it, the other part has eight in it.

1. Tell in your own words when we use the "finding-an-unknown-part" subtraction operation.

2. Write a "finding-an-unknown-part" subtraction story problem for each of these equations. Find the answers.
 a. 28 - 23 = ___   **b.** 43 - 30 = ___   **c.** $0.45 - $0.25 = ___

3. Write a subtraction equation to go with each of these pictures. How many are in the other part?

a.

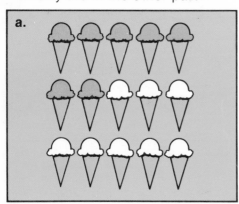

b.

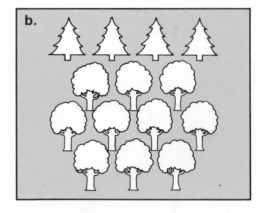

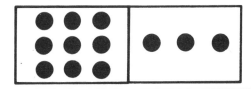

Addition facts	Subtraction facts
9 + 3 = 12	12 - 3 = 9
3 + 9 = 12	12 - 9 = 3

These four facts are related. We can call them a **fact team.**

1. Write fact teams for these sets of numbers.

   a. 7, 8, 15 **b.** 13, 8, 5 **c.** 16, 7, 9 **d.** 8, 14, 6

2. Write the three other facts that are needed to make a complete fact team.

   a. 8 + 9 = 17   **b.** 11 - 5 = 6   **c.** 5 + 9 = 14   **d.** 15 - 6 = 9

3. Give the missing numbers.

   a. 8 + ___ = 11   **f.** ___ = 7 + 8   **k.** 6 + ___ = 9 + 6

   b. 12 - 8 = ___   **g.** 12 = 9 + ___   **l.** 3 + 7 = ___ + 2

   c. ___ + 6 = 13   **h.** 17 = ___ + 9   **m.** 2 + 7 = 12 - ___

   d. ___ - 9 = 5   **i.** 16 = 8 + ___   **n.** ___ - 3 = 15 - 9

   e. 5 + 6 = ___   **j.** 3 = 12 - ___   **o.** ___ + 9 = 17 - 8

Nancy and Barry went to the zoo with their parents. They made a list of some of the animals they saw.

Animals We Saw		
Bears ----✓---- 14	Elephants ----✓ 3	
Big Cats	Alligators ---✓-12	
Tigers ----✓-8	Crocodiles -✓-7	
Lions --✓---12	Deer	
Cheetahs --✓- 3	Moose --✓--- 5	
Leopards --✓- 5	Elk ---✓---14	
Giraffes ----✓-- 7	Mule Deer-20	
Spider Monkeys-15	Whitetails--25	

1. Nancy and Barry saw a total of how many big cats?
2. They saw how many more bears than giraffes?
3. Three of the alligators they saw were on the land and the rest were in the water. How many alligators were in the water?
4. The largest deer Nancy and Barry saw were the moose and the elk. How many of these animals did they see?
5. How many deer did they see altogether?
6. Alligators and crocodiles look very much alike. The children saw a total of how many of these reptiles?
7. A sign on the monkey cage said that the zoo owned twenty-eight spider monkeys. How many more monkeys must be put into the cage with the ones the children saw to have all twenty-eight?
8. Three of the bears the children saw were black bears and the other eleven were brown bears. They saw how many fewer black bears than brown bears?
9. The elephants each weighed about 9,500 pounds. Their total weight was about how many pounds?
10. There is a total of how many animals on the list the children made?

Bible principles

Do you remember what a *principle* is? A principle is a truth. A principle never changes. We can always depend upon it. There are many principles given in the Bible that help Christians know what is right and what is wrong. Read these verses and think about how they can help you do right and avoid evil:

> Obey them that have the rule over you, and submit yourselves: for they watch for your souls, as they that must give account, that they may do it with joy and not with grief; for that is unprofitable for you.
>
> Hebrews 13:17

1. List five persons that have authority over you.
2. Does anyone have authority over your parents?
3. Does anyone have authority over your teachers?
4. Who has authority over everyone and everything?

> And let us not be weary in well doing; for in due season we shall reap, if we faint not.
>
> Galatians 6:9

5. Do you ever get tired of doing homework?
6. Does your mother ever get tired of washing clothes?
7. Does your father ever get tired of going to work?
8. What do you think "keep on keeping on" means?

> These six things doth the Lord hate; yea, seven are an abomination unto Him: a proud look, a lying tongue, and hands that shed innocent blood, an heart that deviseth wicked imaginations, feet that be swift in running to mischief, a false witness that speaketh lies, and he that soweth discord among brethren.
>
> Proverbs 6:16-19

9. Do you want to do something that the Lord hates?
10. What does it mean to devise wicked imaginations?

There are mathematics principles that help us in solving our math problems. These principles are true. They never change. We can always depend on them. You have already learned some of these.

Order Principle for Addition
The order of addends can be changed without changing the sum.

$$5 + 6 = 6 + 5$$

Grouping Principle for Addition
Addends can be grouped in different ways without changing the sum.

$$(3 + 5) + 2 = 3 + (5 + 2)$$

Zero Principle for Addition
When zero is added to a number, the sum is that same number.

$$7 + 0 = 7$$

9 + 4 = ?
I know that 4 + 9 = 13,
so 9 + 4 also equals 13.

What principle is Tom using?

I'll check by adding 3 and 7 first, and then I'll add 5. Yes, 15 is the right answer.

What principle is Lynn using?

A quick way to add

Examine these addition combinations and their sums.

4	14	24	34	44
+ 5	+ 5	+ 5	+ 5	+ 5
9	19	29	39	49

Give the sums aloud. How quickly can you do it?

54	64	74	84	94
+ 5	+ 5	+ 5	+ 5	+ 5

Examine these addition combinations and their sums.

9	19	29	39	49
+ 9	+ 9	+ 9	+ 9	+ 9
18	28	38	48	58

Compare the tens' digit of the first addend and the tens' digit of the sum. What do you notice?

Give the sums aloud. Can you do it quickly?

59	69	79	89	99
+ 9	+ 9	+ 9	+ 9	+ 9

This kind of addition is needed when adding a column of numbers.

```
6 + 8 = 14          6
14 + 5 = 19          8
19 + 9 = 28          5
                   + 9
                    28
```

Notice the addition combinations that are needed to solve this problem. Which ones do you think are the hardest?

Think about the activities you did at the top of the page. Can you figure out a fast way to think of the sums, even of hard combinations?

Adding a one-digit number and a two-digit number

Tim and Heidi are playing a game. Can you figure out
how it is played?

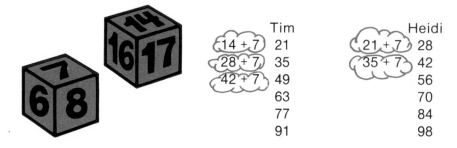

	Tim		Heidi
14 + 7	21	21 + 7	28
28 + 7	35	35 + 7	42
42 + 7	49		56
	63		70
	77		84
	91		98

Heidi won because she gave the sum that was closest
to, but less than, 100.

Write the sums that would be given if these numbers
were rolled.

	Starting number	What to add	First player
2nd game	17	6	Heidi
3rd game	14	9	Tim
4th game	18	7	Heidi
5th game	17	5	Tim
6th game	16	4	Heidi
7th game	19	8	Tim
8th game	15	7	Heidi
9th game	13	9	Tim

If Tim and Heidi rolled these numbers, who was the
winner?

Checking addition

Solve by adding down. Check by adding up.

1.	2.	3.	4.	5.	6.
2	7	3	7	8	3
9	3	8	4	8	7
8	8	6	6	6	2
6	5	2	9	5	9
5	9	8	5	6	8
9	7	3	8	8	1
7	6	7	7	7	6
+ 8	+ 8	+ 9	+ 6	+ 9	+ 8

7.	8.	9.	10.	11.	12.
6	4	9	6	8	9
2	8	3	3	7	8
4	3	8	2	1	7
8	6	9	5	6	2
7	3	4	6	8	7
9	8	5	7	7	3
3	9	3	4	5	7
+ 5	+ 2	+ 7	+ 3	+ 8	+ 4

Do you know why it is important to check your work in
math? What could happen if a mistake is made
    by a person filling out his checkbook?
    by a cook following a recipe?
    by a carpenter sawing boards of a certain length for
     a house?
    by a salesclerk when making out a sales slip?

Renaming in addition

There are 359 elementary students and 168 high school students in Grace Christian School. How many students are there altogether?

$$359 + 168 = \underline{\qquad}$$

Can you explain each step?

Step 1	Step 2	Step 3
$\begin{array}{r} 1 \\ 359 \\ +\ 168 \\ \hline 7 \end{array}$	$\begin{array}{r} 11 \\ 359 \\ +\ 168 \\ \hline 27 \end{array}$	$\begin{array}{r} 1 \\ 359 \\ +\ 168 \\ \hline 527 \end{array}$

There are 527 students in Grace Christian School.

This chart shows the number of lunches sold in Grace Christian School during the first four weeks of school.

	Week 1	Week 2	Week 3	Week 4
Monday	315	290	317	290
Tuesday	300	288	310	331
Wednesday	301	305	295	274
Thursday	294	275	328	289
Friday	318	413	284	400

1. What was the total number of lunches sold for each week?

2. What was the total number of lunches sold for all four weeks?

3. Solve.

a.	b.	c.	d.	e.
$\begin{array}{r} 39 \\ 24 \\ +\ 68 \\ \hline \end{array}$	$\begin{array}{r} 47 \\ 79 \\ +\ 26 \\ \hline \end{array}$	$\begin{array}{r} 65 \\ 93 \\ +\ 79 \\ \hline \end{array}$	$\begin{array}{r} 78 \\ 26 \\ +\ 97 \\ \hline \end{array}$	$\begin{array}{r} 86 \\ 38 \\ +\ 56 \\ \hline \end{array}$

Column addition

Four children took trips during the month of September. This chart shows the number of miles each traveled. What was the total number of miles traveled?

Child	Miles
Pam	325
Jon	75
Kent	1,236
Amy	206

Numbers to be added	Step 1 Arrange ones, tens, hundreds, and thousands in columns.	Step 2 Add.
325 75 1,236 206	325 75 1,236 206	325 75 1,236 + 206

Add each set of numbers.

1. 46   392   5,064

2. 8   745   925

3. 72   459   9

4. 5,614   8   456   34

5. 7   682   4,314   85

6. 298   81   2,937   7   49

7. 15   2,463   528

8. 461   14   8

9. 4,643   92   5

10. 7,463   15   424

11. 3,468   18   500

12. 427   18   916

29

Renaming in subtraction

There are 452 books in the library in Miss Smith's fourth grade classroom. Last week the class checked out 38 of the books. How many books were left?

$$452 - 38 = \underline{\quad}$$

Can you explain each step?

Step 1	Step 2	Step 3	Step 4
4 12 4̶5̶2̶ - 38	4 12 4̶5̶2̶ - 38 ─── 4	4 12 4̶5̶2̶ - 38 ─── 14	4 12 4̶5̶2̶ - 38 ─── 414

There were 414 books not checked out.

1. Solve.

a. 192	**b.** 153	**c.** 675	**d.** 383	**e.** 675
- 168	- 29	- 148	- 247	- 268

Some of the books in Miss Smith's classroom were paperbacks. There were 191 paperbacks and 261 hardbacks. There were how many fewer paperback books than hardback books?

$$261 - 191 = \underline{\quad}$$

Can you explain each step?

Step 1	Step 2	Step 3
261 - 191 ─── 0	1 16 2̶6̶1̶ - 191 ─── 0	1 16 2̶6̶1̶ - 191 ─── 70

There were 70 fewer paperback books.

2. Solve.

a. 435	**b.** 726	**c.** 324	**d.** 537	**e.** 628
- 182	- 594	- 83	- 253	- 295

There are 263 students in Heritage Christian School. This year 89 of the students are taking music lessons. How many students are not taking music lessons?

$263 - 89 = \underline{\hspace{2cm}}$

Can you explain each step?

Step 1	Step 2	Step 3	Step 4	Step 5
5 13 2̶6̶3̶ - 89	5 13 2̶6̶3̶ - 89 4	1 15 13 2̶6̶3̶ - 89 4	1 15 13 2̶6̶3̶ - 89 74	1 15 13 2̶6̶3̶ - 89 174

There are 174 students who are not taking music lessons.

1. Solve.

a. 315
- 178

b. 725
- 349

c. 263
- 94

d. 3,226
- 1,668

e. 3,273
- 2,187

God's Word commands Christians to examine (or check) themselves to make sure they are living in a way that pleases the Lord. God is interested in everything we do. That means He is interested in how we do our math problems. I Corinthians 10:31b says, "Whatsoever ye do, do all to the glory of God."

Do you remember how to check subtraction problems?

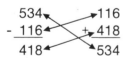

```
  534         116
- 116       + 418
  418         534
```

2. Solve and check.

a. 735
- 486

b. 624
- 287

c. 445
- 376

d. 5,315
- 1,787

e. 82,149
- 65,268

Phil and his sister Cindy collect animal cards. They sorted them and made a chart to show how many they had of each kind.

Kind of animal	Number
Insects	95
Fish	60
Birds	138
Mammals	245
Other	78

1. How many cards did they have altogether?

2. Cindy keeps the insect and the bird cards in her room. How many cards does Cindy have?

3. If Phil keeps the rest of the cards, who has the most cards? How many more cards does that person have?

Phil found this information while he was reading his mammal cards.

Animal	Life Span	Adult Weight
Black Bear	26 years	up to 550 lb.
Elephant	55 years	up to 9,500 lb.
Lion	25 years	up to 420 lb.
Camel	55 years	up to 1,520 lb.
Walrus	30 years	up to 4,800 lb.

4. The elephant's life span is how many years longer than the life span of a lion?

5. A black bear's life span is how much less than the life span of a camel?

6. A large elephant will weigh about how much more than a large walrus?

7. A large lion will weigh about how much less than a large black bear?

8. Solve.

    a. 523 **b.** 7,185 **c.** 5,540 **d.** 9,142 **e.** 75,620
       - 167   - 4,293   - 1,865   - 3,850   - 29,918

Jim used an abacus to show his class how he solved this problem.

500 - 168 = _____

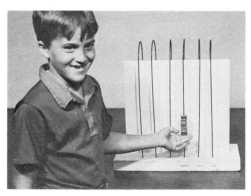

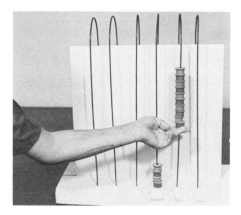

I want to subtract
8 ones but I do not
have any ones.
I will try to **rename**
a ten. I have no tens.

```
  500
- 168
```

I will rename a
hundred as 10 tens.
Now I have 4 hun-
dreds and 10 tens.

```
  4 10
  5̶0̶0
- 168
```

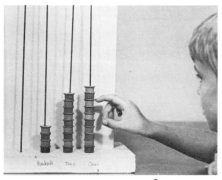

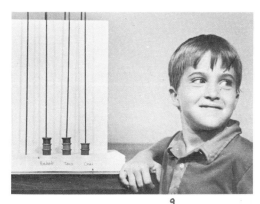

I will rename a ten
as 10 ones. I have
4 hundreds, 9 tens,
and 10 ones.

```
     9
  4 1̶0̶ 10
  5̶0̶0̶
- 168
```

Now I can subtract.
I have 332 left.

```
     9
  4 1̶0̶ 10
  5̶0̶0̶
- 168
  332
```

Explain what was done in each of these problems.

```
     9              9              9
  5 1̶0̶ 10        8 1̶0̶ 10        7 1̶0̶ 12
  6̶0̶0̶            9̶0̶0̶            8̶0̶2̶
- 247          - 463          - 598
  353            437            204
```

Practice

$$\begin{array}{r} {\scriptstyle 3\,10} \\ 4\!\!\!/0\!\!\!/0 \\ -\ 123 \end{array}$$

a. Why was the 4 crossed off and a 3 written above it?
b. What does the 10 mean?

$$\begin{array}{r} {\scriptstyle 3\,\overset{9}{\cancel{10}}10} \\ 4\!\!\!/0\!\!\!/0 \\ -\ 123 \end{array}$$

c. What does the 9 mean?
d. Why was a 10 written in the ones' place?

$$\begin{array}{r} {\scriptstyle 3\,\overset{9}{\cancel{10}}10} \\ 4\!\!\!/0\!\!\!/0 \\ -\ 123 \\ \hline 277 \end{array}$$

e. How can you check this answer?

Solve.

1. 500 - 263	**2.** 600 - 417	**3.** 405 - 188	**4.** 800 - 264	**5.** 300 - 126
6. 904 - 467	**7.** 200 - 89	**8.** 503 - 376	**9.** 700 - 418	**10.** 307 - 199
11. 600 - 354	**12.** 300 - 185	**13.** 901 - 364	**14.** 800 - 246	**15.** 700 - 439
16. 202 - 178	**17.** 500 - 387	**18.** 707 - 256	**19.** 801 - 547	**20.** 600 - 278
21. 3,004 - 1,268	**22.** 8,000 - 6,342	**23.** 20,700 - 18,900	**24.** 6,008 - 4,528	**25.** 90,500 - 36,826

Subtraction with money

Kathy bought a book for $2.15. She gave the clerk a five-dollar bill. How much change did she receive?

$5.00 - $2.15 = _____

$5.00
- 2.15
$2.85

She received $2.85.

Solve.

1.	$ 6.00	2.	$ 8.00	3.	$ 4.00	4.	$ 1.00	5.	$ 9.00
	- 2.56		- 3.45		- 3.63		- 0.32		- 5.89

6.	$ 20.04	7.	$ 70.00	8.	$ 50.08	9.	$100.00	10.	$500.00
	- 6.19		- 5.08		- 14.52		- 92.88		- 313.10

Subtract to 495

1. Choose any three digits.   2   6   8

2. Make the greatest and the least three-digit numbers from them that you can.   862 and 268

3. Subtract.
862
- 268
594

4. Make the greatest and the least three-digit numbers from the digits in the answer.   954 and 459

5. Subtract.
954
- 459
495

The difference is 495. You subtracted two times.

Try other sets of three digits. How many times must you subtract before your answer is 495?

a. 7   3   5   **c.** 3   9   0
b. 5   1   8   **d.** You choose the digits.

Have you ever been in a store and wanted to find the total cost of two or more items, but you didn't have pencil and paper along? Were you able to add the prices in your mind?

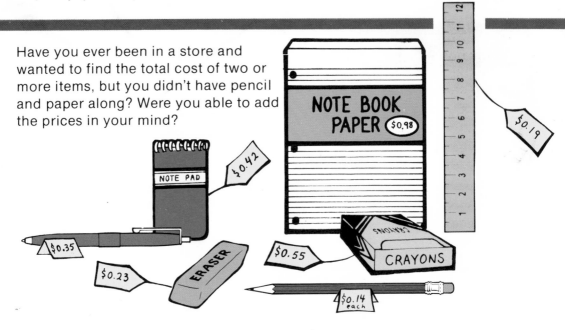

1. Find the total cost of these items by just thinking about it.

   a. pencil and eraser   **b.** notepad and pen   **c.** crayons and notepad

Bill knows a way to add 19¢ and 42¢ in his mind.

2. Find the cost of these items. Do not write the problem.

   a. eraser   **b.** notebook paper   **c.** ruler   **d.** ruler
      ruler   eraser   pen   crayons

Addition practice

Do you remember the practice pages in your third grade math book that were taken from a math book printed in 1868? Here is a page of addition practice from that same book.

70   PRIMARY ARITHMETIC.

Addition is the process of finding the sum of two or more numbers.

The number obtained by adding two or more numbers is called the *Sum*.

WRITTEN EXERCISES.

	(1)	(2)	(3)	(4)		(1)	(2)	(3)	(4)	(5)	(6)
	19	29	39	49		9	2	3	9	3	4
Add	44	36	28	12		9	2	2	3	9	9
						9	9	3	9	4	5

	(1)	(2)	(3)	(4)		9	2	9	4	5	9
	14	5	13	14		9	9	3	9	9	6
	15	14	22	15		9	9	9	9	9	9
	24	13	19	16		9	9	9	9	9	9
	23	25	16	18		9	9	9	9	9	9
Add	19	39	29	29	Add	9	2	3	4	5	6

LESSON XLII.

WRITTEN EXERCISES IN ADDITION

Copy and add the following examples:

(1)	(2)	(3)	(4)	(5)	(6)	(7)	(8)	(9)	10)
2	3	3	2	3	7	8	6	3	8
3	2	4	3	6	5	3	3	9	6
1	3	2	5	5	4	8	9	4	4
2	2	3	4	3	6	4	3	9	2
3	3	2	5	4	3	5	4	8	1
2	1	4	3	2	7	8	9	2	3
3	2	3	2	1	6	7	8	1	5
2	3	4	5	6	5	3	7	3	7
3	2	3	1	5	4	6	2	9	9
1	1	1	5	3	3	2	3	4	2

(11)	(12)	(13)	(14)	(15)	(16)	(17)	(18)
22	13	24	25	28	16	25	17
32	34	25	27	15	29	26	38
24	22	16	18	24	28	19	15
21	27	34	29	27	27	27	26

1. What are two things we can learn about God by looking at what He has made?

2. Why is our number system sometimes called the Hindu-Arabic system?

3. Write in expanded form: **a.** 275   **b.** 3,678   **c.** 1,000,209

4. Write the greatest three-digit numeral possible using these digits.   4, 9, 5

5. Write the following in standard form.
   a. ten thousand, sixty-four   **b.** one million, one hundred fifty
   c. three hundred thousand, two hundred nine

6. Tell what the 5 means in each numeral.
   a. 32,516   **b.** 5,417   **c.** 12,536,142

7. Write a story problem that would be solved by this equation: 64 + 38 = _____.

8. Write a "comparing" story problem that would be solved by this equation: 32 - 28 = _____.

9. Solve.
   a. 36 + 95 + 83 + 79 =   **d.** 814 - 138 =
   b. 952 + 85 + 315 + 7 =   **e.** 700 - 263 =
   c. 4,375 + 1,269 + 483 + 2,856 =   **f.** $90.00 - $18.35 =

10. Bill needed to know the sum of 2 + 7 but he did not remember what it was. He thought of 7 + 2 and knew the sum he needed was 9. What math principle did Bill use?

11. Explain in your own words how to check a subtraction problem.

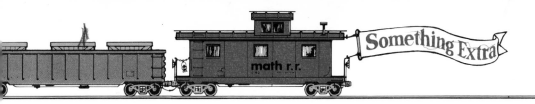

Something Extra

1	5	10	50	100	500	1,000
I	V	X	L	C	D	M

Can you figure out the pattern that is used to write these roman numerals?

Ones
1 I
2 II
3 III
4 IV
5 V
6 VI
7 VII
8 VIII
9 IX
10 X

Tens
10 X
20 XX
30 XXX
40 XL
50 L
60 LX
70 LXX
80 LXXX
90 XC
100 C

1. Write from 100 to 1,000 by hundreds, using roman numerals.

To find the roman numeral for 364:
364 = 300 + 60 + 4
        CCC + LX + IV
364 = CCCLXIV

To find the Hindu-Arabic numeral for MCCXIII:
MCCXIII =   M + CC + X + III
               1,000 + 200 + 10 + 3
MCCXIII = 1,213

2. Give the roman numerals.

a. 38	**b.** 153	**c.** 625	**d.** 1,050
e. 88	**f.** 634	**g.** 569	**h.** 520
i. 694	**j.** 1,982		

3. Give the Hindu-Arabic numerals.

a. XXXI	**b.** CCL	**c.** LXVII	**d.** XCIV
e. XVIII	**f.** MCXI	**g.** DLXXIV	**h.** XCIII
i. CCVII	**j.** MMVI		

Unit 2

The Johnstown Flood

The sound of rain outside a passenger car usually makes the warm, dry people inside want to curl up and sleep. But on the morning of May 31, 1889, no one felt like sleeping. The spring rains had filled the Conemaugh River too full. The people on the train that ran alongside the river could see that it was now out of its banks. They also knew that the water was weakening the dam at Lake Conemaugh ahead of them. If the dam broke, millions of gallons of muddy water would rush down the valley and bury the town of East Conemaugh, the city of Johnstown, and everything in between them.

The people on the train were now between those two towns. Suddenly they heard the signal that the dam had broken. Immediately the train stopped and the people on board were told to climb the hill nearby. The people quickly got off the train and started to run toward the hill, but between the train and the hill was a deep ditch. Twenty-six people died because they could not get across the ditch. They had been warned about the danger. They had tried to escape, but the ditch kept them from safety.

Many people today have heard about salvation and might even consider being saved. Unfortunately, they know someone who claims to be a Christian but who lives a very sinful life. His life is like the ditch that kept the people from safety. But he does more than destroy the lives of those involved. He destroys their souls. (See Matthew 23:13.)

Goals for Unit 2

1. I will understand the multiplication operation.
2. I will understand the division operation.
3. I will know all the multiplication and division facts.
4. I will know the order principle for multiplication and the multiplication-addition principle.
5. I will learn the meaning of cross-product multiplication.
6. I will learn how to multiply two- or three-digit numbers.

Words to Remember

factor

product

divisor

dividend

quotient

multiplication-addition principle

partial products

cross-product multiplication

pictograph

What do you remember?

1. Write an addition equation and a multiplication equation to tell how many circles there are altogether.

○○○○○ ○○○○○ ○○○○○ ○○○○○

2. Write multiplication equations for these products.
   a. 32 **b.** 56 **c.** 42 **d.** 27 **e.** 72

3. If you forget what 4 × 9 equals, what are two ways you could find the answer?

4. Solve.
   a. 7 × 5 = **b.** 8 × 6 = **c.** 6 × 6 = **d.** 9 × 7 = **e.** 8 × 5 =

5. Draw a picture to show the answer to 15 ÷ 3 = ____.

6. If you forget what 27 ÷ 3 equals, what are two ways you could find the answer?

7. Give the quotients.
   a. 54 ÷ 6 = **b.** 45 ÷ 5 = **c.** 28 ÷ 7 = **d.** 18 ÷ 3 = **e.** 24 ÷ 3 =

8. Find the quotients and the remainders.
   a. 7)60 **b.** 6)58 **c.** 5)43 **d.** 8)27 **e.** 3)19

9. Write two multiplication facts and two division facts using the numbers 6, 60, and 10.

10. Write an equation for each problem. Solve.
    a. Jim put six pictures on each page of his picture album. He has put forty-eight pictures in the album altogether. How many pages has he used?

    b. Trixie read four books about birds each week for five weeks. How many books about birds did Trixie read during those weeks?

A classroom has four rows of desks with seven desks in each row. How many desks are there altogether?

$$7 + 7 + 7 + 7 = 28$$

or

$$4 \times 7 = 28$$

factors   product

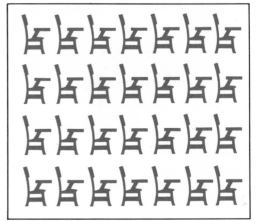

This is a multiplication equation. It tells us that when four sets of seven are joined together, a set of twenty-eight is made.

1. Tell in your own words when to use the multiplication operation.

2. What does the first factor of a multiplication equation tell? What does the second factor tell? What does the product tell?

3. Write a story problem for each of these equations. Find the answers.

   a. $5 \times 9 =$ _____   **b.** $7 \times 8 =$ _____   **c.** $8 \times \$0.10 =$ _____

4. Write an equation to be used to find how many objects there are altogether in each of these pictures.

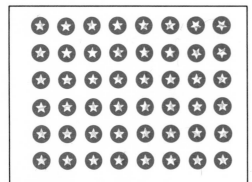
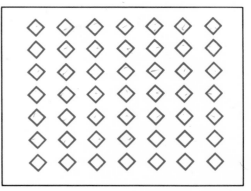

Addition and multiplication are related

1. Write an addition equation and a multiplication equation for each drawing.

a.

b.

c.

d.

2. Make a drawing to go with each equation.
   a. $2 \times 4 = 8$ **b.** $3 \times 2 = 6$ **c.** $4 \times 5 = 20$ **d.** $5 \times 1 = 5$

3. Write a multiplication equation for each of the following. (Make a drawing to help you find the answers if necessary.)
   a. 3 sets of 9   **b.** 6 sets of 2   **c.** 4 sets of 6

   d. 8 sets of 4   **e.** 7 sets of 5   **f.** 6 sets of 7

We can write a multiplication fact two ways.

$$8 \times 3 = 24$$

They are both read, "Eight times three equals twenty-four."

4. Copy and complete.

a.	**b.**	**c.**	**d.**	**e.**	**f.**
6	8	3	5	4	3
× 4	× 5	× 7	× 5	× 5	× 9

$3 \times 6 = 18$ $6 \times 3 = 18$

Notice the order of the factors in these equations.

Notice the products in these equations.

Order Principle
The order of the factors in a multiplication equation can be changed without changing the product.

I don't remember what 5×3 equals, but I know that 3×5 equals 15.

Tammy uses this math principle to help her remember some of the multiplication facts.

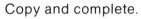

Copy and complete.

1. Since $9 \times 4 = 36$, then $4 \times 9 = $ _____
2. Since $8 \times 5 = 40$, then $5 \times 8 = $ _____
3. Since $6 \times 4 = 24$, then ___ × ___ = _____
4. Since $9 \times 5 = 45$, then ___ × ___ = _____
5. Since $8 \times 4 = 32$, then ___ × ___ = _____
6. Since $7 \times 5 = 35$, then ___ × ___ = _____
7. Since $6 \times 9 = 54$, then ___ × ___ = _____
8. Since $8 \times 7 = 56$, then ___ × ___ = _____
9. Since $8 \times 9 = 72$, then ___ × ___ = _____
10. Since $6 \times 7 = 42$, then ___ × ___ = _____

Thinking about multiplication

Finding the answer to multiplication facts is important. It is also important to know how to use multiplication facts to solve real problems.

1. You know that 5 × 7 has the same product as 7 × 5. Is buying 5 items that cost 7¢ each the same as buying 7 items that cost 5¢ each? Would it make a difference in the amount of money you would pay? Would it make a difference in the number of items that you take home?   .

2. You know that 6 × 4 = 4 × 6. Is 6 cars with 4 people in each the same as 4 cars with 6 people in each? Are there the same number of people in each situation?

3. You know that 2 × 8 = 8 × 2. Is learning 8 Bible verses a day for 2 days the same as learning 2 verses a day for 8 days? Would the number of verses be the same? Which would you rather do?

4. Write the correct multiplication equation for each of the problems below. What does the first factor tell? What does the second factor tell?

   a. Bill has four bags with six apples in each bag. How many apples does he have?
   b. Oranges cost six cents each. What will seven oranges cost?
   c. There are five shelves of books with ten books on each shelf. How many books are there in all?
   d. Cindy made three dresses for each of her four dolls. How many dresses did she make?
   e. Tim bought six packages of gum. There were five sticks in each package. How many sticks of gum did he buy?

	0	1	2	3	4	5	6	7	8	9	10
0	0	0	0	0	0	0	0	0	0	0	0
1	0	1	2	3	4	5	6	7	8	9	10
2	0	2	4	6	8	10	12	14	16	18	20
3	0	3	6	9	12	15	18	21	24	27	30
4	0	4	8	12	16	20	24	28	32	36	40
5	0	5	10	15	20	25	30	35	40	45	50
6	0	6	12	18	24	30	36	42	48	54	60
7	0	7	14	21	28	35	42	49	56	63	70
8	0	8	16	24	32	40	48	56	64	72	80
9	0	9	18	27	36	45	54	63	72	81	90
10	0	10	20	30	40	50	60	70	80	90	100

This multiplication table contains the products of all the facts from 0 × 0 through 10 × 10. Find the product of 4 × 3. There are 121 products shown on this table. This means that there are 121 facts that you must know. You know many of these facts already.

1. What is the product of all multiplication facts that have 0 as a factor? Notice that these products are on colored squares. You do not need to memorize these facts.

2. What do you know about all multiplication facts that have 1 as a factor? Do you have to study these facts?

3. Why are the facts 2 × 2 = ___ , 2 × 3 = ___ , 2 × 4 = ___ ... 2 × 10 = ___ so easy to remember? You probably do not need to study these.

4. Since 2 × 3 = 6, then 3 × 2 = 6. Since 2 × 4 = 8, then
   4 × 2 = ___. Do you have to study these facts: 3 × 2 = 6,
   4 × 2 = 8, ... 10 × 2 = 20?

5. Find the products of 3 × 3, 3 × 4, 3 × 5, ... 3 × 10. You
   must study these until you know them. After you
   know these, you should not need to study these facts:
   4 × 3 = 12, 5 × 3 = 15, ... 10 × 3 = 30. Why?

6. Find the products of 4 × 4, 4 × 5, ... 4 × 10. After you
   have learned these, what facts should you know
   also?

7. Do the same thing with 5, 6, 7, 8, 9, and 10.

8. Notice that on the multiplication table all the products
   you should not have to study are on colored squares.
   The ones you must memorize are on white squares.
   How many are on white squares?

Set a goal! When will you have the multiplication facts
learned?

Ginger uses another mathematical principle to help her think of some products she has forgotten.

6 × 9 = ?
I will think of
6 × 5 and 6 × 4.

6 × 5 = 30   6 × 4 = 24

30 + 24 = 54
6 × 9 = 54

Steps in Using the Multiplication-Addition Principle
1. Separate a factor into parts.
2. Multiply each of the parts by the other factor.
3. Add those **partial products** to find the total product.

4 × 8 =	6 × 7 =	4 × 9 =
4 × (3 + 5) =	(3 + 3) × 7 =	4 × (3 + 6) =
(4 × 3) + (4 × 5) =	(3 × 7) + (3 × 7) =	(4 × 3) + (4 × 6) =
12 + 20 =	21 + 21 =	12 + 24 =

Use the multiplication-addition principle to find the answers to these facts.

a. 7 × 8 = ___   **b.** 6 × 8 = ___   **c.** 9 × 7 = ___   **d.** 8 × 8 = ___

50

More multiplication facts

It is important to memorize all the multiplication facts. They will help you solve problems quickly. Perhaps you have not learned the facts with factors of eleven and twelve. Examine the tables below. You will see that these facts are easy to remember.

0 × 11 = 0	7 × 11 = 77
1 × 11 = 11	8 × 11 = 88
2 × 11 = 22	9 × 11 = 99
3 × 11 = 33	10 × 11 = 110
4 × 11 = 44	11 × 11 = 121
5 × 11 = 55	12 × 11 = 132
6 × 11 = 66	

0 × 12 = 0	7 × 12 = 84
1 × 12 = 12	8 × 12 = 96
2 × 12 = 24	9 × 12 = 108
3 × 12 = 36	10 × 12 = 120
4 × 12 = 48	11 × 12 = 132
5 × 12 = 60	12 × 12 = 144
6 × 12 = 72	

Write as many facts as possible that have these products.
(Example: 16   2 × 8, 8 × 2, 4 × 4)

1.	12	**2.**	18	**3.**	24	**4.**	48
5.	36	**6.**	60	**7.**	49	**8.**	16
9.	72	**10.**	40	**11.**	42	**12.**	28

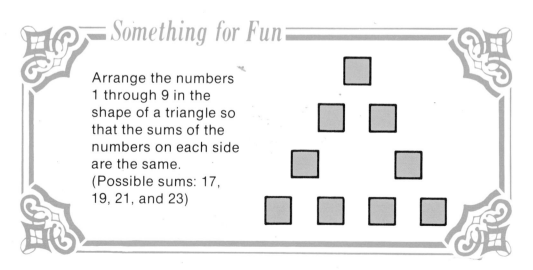

Something for Fun

Arrange the numbers 1 through 9 in the shape of a triangle so that the sums of the numbers on each side are the same.
(Possible sums: 17, 19, 21, and 23)

Sandwiches	Drinks
Hot dog	Milk
Hamburger	Orange juice
Toasted cheese	

Each student in Miss Lee's class ordered a sandwich and something to drink for lunch. These are the choices that were possible.

Hot dog and milk	Hot dog and orange juice
Hamburger and milk	Hamburger and orange juice
Toasted cheese and milk	Toasted cheese and orange juice

How many choices were there?

Ice cream	Topping
Vanilla	Chocolate
Chocolate	Strawberry
Strawberry	Marshmallow
	Butterscotch

Each student also ordered ice cream with topping. What were the possible choices (with one kind of ice cream and one topping for each student)? How many choices were there? 12.

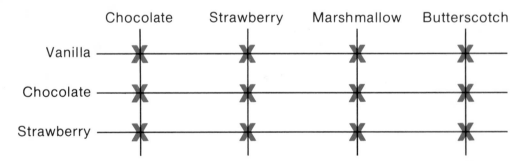

Find the answers. Make a drawing to help you.

1. What combinations can
   Mr. Hunt make?
   How many combinations
   are possible?

Shirt	Tie
white	striped
tan	plain
brown	dotted

2. What combinations can
   Lisa make?
   How many combinations
   are possible?

Coat	Scarf
blue	white
tan	red
	striped

3. What combinations can
   the campers have?
   How many combinations
   are possible?

Morning Activity	Afternoon Activity
archery	swimming
crafts	riflery
soccer	boating
trail blazing	

4. You can use multiplication to find how many
   combinations are possible in each of these situations.

   a. Mr. Hunt had how many shirts? He had how many
      ties? He had how many choices?
   b. Lisa had how many coats? She had how many
      scarves? She had how many combinations?
   c. The campers had how many choices for the
      morning activity class? They had how many
      choices for the afternoon activity class? They had
      how many combinations of classes?

5. How are these multiplication equations different from
   the problems on page 44?

This kind of multiplication is often called **cross-product
multiplication.**

Write a multiplication equation for each problem. Solve.

1. Jack has four pairs of trousers and six shirts. How many different outfits can he wear?

2. Four students are running for class president and three are running for vice-president. How many different sets of officers could be elected?

3. A store has five kinds of paper and eight colors of ribbon that can be used to wrap gifts. How many different combinations can be made?

4. Barbara has eleven dolls and six stuffed animals. She may take one doll and one animal with her on vacation. How many possible combinations can she make?

5. Write a story problem to go with this equation: $2 \times 4 =$ _____. Use cross-product multiplication.

6. List the ways to get to the throne.

7. What is the fast way to find how many ways there are to get to the throne?

54

1. Read aloud. Complete each equation as you read.

a. 2 × 1 =
 2 × 10 =
 2 × 100 =
 2 × 1,000 =

b. 5 × 1 =
 5 × 10 =
 5 × 100 =
 5 × 1,000 =

c. 9 × 1 =
 9 × 10 =
 9 × 100 =
 9 × 1,000 =

d. 2 × 2 =
 2 × 20 =
 2 × 200 =
 2 × 2,000 =

e. 5 × 2 =
 5 × 20 =
 5 × 200 =
 5 × 2,000 =

f. 9 × 2 = 18
 9 × 20 = 180
 9 × 200 = 1,800
 9 × 2,000 = 18,000

g. 2 × 5 =
 2 × 50 =
 2 × 500 =
 2 × 5,000 =

h. 5 × 5 =
 5 × 50 =
 5 × 500 =
 5 × 5,000 =

i. 9 × 5 =
 9 × 50 =
 9 × 500 =
 9 × 5,000 =

2. Write an equation for each problem. Solve.

   a. How many pieces are in eight boxes of chalk?

   b. How many paper clips are in six boxes?

   c. How many sheets of art paper are in five packages?

   d. How many sheets of notebook paper are in seven packages?

   e. How many crayons are in nine boxes?

   f. How many rubber bands are in eight boxes?

These boxes each contain 30 cookies. How many cookies are in the three boxes?

$3 \times 30 =$ ____

Step 1		Step 2	
30 × 3 —— 0	There are no ones, so write 0 in the ones' place.	30 × 3 —— 90	3 sets of 3 tens is 9 tens. Write 9 in the tens' place.

1. Solve.

   a. 20   **b.** 30   **c.** 40   **d.** 60   **e.** 70
     × 4   × 2   × 3   × 4   × 5

These boxes each contain 21 cookies. How many cookies are in the three boxes?

$3 \times 21 =$ ____

Step 1		Step 2	
21 × 3 —— 3	3 sets of 1 is 3. Write 3 in the ones' place.	21 × 3 —— 63	3 sets of 2 tens is 6 tens. Write 6 in the tens' place.

2. Solve.

   a. 22   **b.** 41   **c.** 43   **d.** 52   **e.** 31
     × 4   × 2   × 3   × 4   × 6

Multiplication with renaming

These boxes of cookies each contain 24 cookies. How many cookies are in the three boxes?

3 × 24 = _____

You can use the multiplication-addition principle to help you find the answer.

3 sets of 4	3 sets of 20	3 sets of 24
4 × 3 ___ 12	20 × 3 ___ 60	60 + 12 ___ 72

There is a short way to write this.

Step 1

24
× 3
___
2.

3 sets of 4 is 12. Write 2 in the ones' place. Remember the extra ten.

Step 2

24
× 3
___
72

3 sets of 2 tens is 6 tens. Add the extra ten to make 7 tens. Write 7 in the tens' place.

Solve.

1. 26
    × 5

2. 34
    × 3

3. 26
    × 4

4. 53
    × 5

5. 37
    × 2

6. 24
    × 4

7. 18
    × 3

8. 46
    × 3

9. 43
    × 5

10. 63
    × 3

11. 47
    × 3

12. 64
    × 4

13. 16
    × 3

14. 58
    × 2

15. 73
    × 4

1. Solve.

a. 38 × 4	**b.** 56 × 5	**c.** 37 × 8	**d.** 29 × 3	**e.** 89 × 4
f. 74 × 7	**g.** 82 × 6	**h.** 59 × 9	**i.** 73 × 5	**j.** 94 × 8
k. 35 × 3	**l.** 49 × 8	**m.** 82 × 7	**n.** 54 × 6	**o.** 43 × 7

2. Solve.

a. $0.16 × 5	**b.** $0.35 × 2	**c.** $0.19 × 4	**d.** $0.32 × 3	**e.** $0.24 × 4
f. $0.63 × 2	**g.** $0.35 × 4	**h.** $0.52 × 6	**i.** $0.29 × 8	**j.** $0.37 × 5
k. $0.28 × 3	**l.** $0.59 × 5	**m.** $0.76 × 8	**n.** $0.32 × 4	**o.** $0.52 × 7

3. Write a story problem for each of these equations. Solve.

a. $4 \times \$1.25 =$ ___   **b.** $3 \times 68 =$ ___   **c.** $7 \times 44 =$ ___

1. Find the cost.

    a. three Big 0's

    b. five Fishwiches

    c. six Connorburgers
        with cheese

    d. two large soft drinks

    e. six small soft drinks

    f. four fries

    g. two Big O's, two fries, and two medium soft drinks

    h. three Connorburgers, two fries, and three small soft drinks

    i. four Connor dogs, two medium soft drinks, two large soft drinks

    j. You have $1.50. You want a sandwich, fries, and a soft drink. What are three combinations you could have? How much change would you get from each?

2. Complete these tables.

×	12
6	
8	
5	
7	
10	
4	

×	9
8	
9	
7	
6	
12	
5	

×	11
8	
12	
11	
9	
10	
7	

Multiplying three-digit numbers

The speed of the Turboliner was 125 miles per hour. How far could that train travel in five hours?

5 × 125 = _____

Step 1

$$\begin{array}{r} \overset{2}{125} \\ \times\ 5 \\ \hline 5 \end{array}$$

5 sets of 5 ones is 25 ones. Write 5 in the ones' place. Remember the 2 tens.

Step 2

$$\begin{array}{r} \overset{1\,2}{125} \\ \times\ 5 \\ \hline 25 \end{array}$$

5 sets of 2 tens is 10 tens; add the extra 2 tens. Rename the 12 tens as 1 hundred and 2 tens. Write 2 in the tens' place. Remember the 1 hundred.

Step 3

$$\begin{array}{r} \overset{1\,2}{125} \\ \times\ 5 \\ \hline 625 \end{array}$$

5 sets of 1 hundred is 5 hundreds. Add the extra 1 hundred. Write 6 in the hundreds' place.

Explain how these examples were solved.

$$\begin{array}{r} 265 \\ \times\ 5 \\ \hline 1{,}325 \end{array} \qquad \begin{array}{r} 407 \\ \times\ 8 \\ \hline 3{,}256 \end{array} \qquad \begin{array}{r} 960 \\ \times\ 5 \\ \hline 4{,}800 \end{array}$$

Solve.

1. $\begin{array}{r} 232 \\ \times\ 4 \\ \hline \end{array}$
2. $\begin{array}{r} 409 \\ \times\ 3 \\ \hline \end{array}$
3. $\begin{array}{r} 563 \\ \times\ 3 \\ \hline \end{array}$
4. $\begin{array}{r} 173 \\ \times\ 5 \\ \hline \end{array}$
5. $\begin{array}{r} 248 \\ \times\ 4 \\ \hline \end{array}$

6. $\begin{array}{r} 512 \\ \times\ 7 \\ \hline \end{array}$
7. $\begin{array}{r} 825 \\ \times\ 4 \\ \hline \end{array}$
8. $\begin{array}{r} 109 \\ \times\ 2 \\ \hline \end{array}$
9. $\begin{array}{r} 328 \\ \times\ 4 \\ \hline \end{array}$
10. $\begin{array}{r} 560 \\ \times\ 6 \\ \hline \end{array}$

Multiply.

1. 8 times the number of days in Genesis 7:24

2. 4 times the number of servants in Genesis 14:14

3. 5 times the number of palm trees in Exodus 15:27

4. 3 times the number of taches in Exodus 26:6

5. 7 times the number of men in Joshua 7:5

6. 2 times the number of men in Judges 3:31

7. 6 times the number of foxes in Judges 15:4

8. 8 times the number of days in I Samuel 17:16

9. 5 times the number of children in II Kings 2:24

10. 9 times the number of cubits in Esther 5:14

11. $5 \times 26 =$ **16.** $4 \times 144 =$

12. $7 \times 14 =$ **17.** $3 \times 296 =$

13. $9 \times 27 =$ **18.** $2 \times 275 =$

14. $8 \times 63 =$ **19.** $4 \times 164 =$

15. $5 \times 87 =$ **20.** $8 \times 635 =$

Solving problems

1. There are eight tables in the lunchroom. Each table is large enough for twenty-two children. How many children can be seated at one time?

2. Mrs. Baker bought seven bags of oranges. Each bag weighed twenty-six pounds. How many pounds of oranges did she buy?

3. Each crate holds 216 cartons of milk. How many cartons of milk will be in two full crates?

4. Mrs. Baker bought two bags of sweet potatoes and four bags of white potatoes. Each bag held fifty pounds. What was the total weight of the potatoes?

5. One loaf of bread will make twelve sandwiches. Mrs. Baker has nine loaves of bread. How many sandwiches can she make?

6. One large can of soup mix can be made into soup for fifteen servings. How many servings can be made from eight large cans of mix?

7. Mrs. Baker has eight boxes of drinking straws. There are five hundred straws in each box. She has a total of how many straws?

8. One box of cake mix makes twenty-eight cupcakes. Mrs. Baker used four boxes of chocolate cake mix and three boxes of banana cake mix. How many cupcakes could she make?

9. A carton of milk costs $0.12. How much will it cost to buy one carton each day for five days?

10. A lunch costs $0.75. How much will five lunches cost?

Mrs. Croft bought 125 boxes of pencils. There were five pencils in each box. How many pencils did Mrs. Croft buy altogether?

125 × 5 = ___

Which of these do you think would be easier to solve?

$$\begin{array}{r} 5 \\ \times\ 125 \\ \hline \end{array} \qquad \begin{array}{r} 125 \\ \times\ 5 \\ \hline \end{array}$$

What math principle helps us to know that 125 × 5 = 5 × 125?

When solving multiplication problems, we sometimes apply the order principle to make our work easier.

Write an equation for each of these problems.
Solve each problem in the easiest way.

1. Tom sold forty-seven boxes of light bulbs. There were five bulbs in each box. How many light bulbs did he sell in all?
2. Mrs. Cox gave three sheets of paper to each of her twenty-seven pupils. She gave out a total of how many sheets of paper?
3. A grocer had seven bags of apples. There were fifteen apples in each bag. How many apples were there altogether?
4. Trina put 5¢ in the Sunday school offering every Sunday for a year (52 weeks). How much did she give that year?
5. A box of chalk holds 144 pieces. How many pieces of chalk are in six boxes?

Here are twenty-four buttons. If we put three on a card, how many cards do we need?

$$\underline{\hspace{1cm}} \times 3 = 24$$

or

$$24 \div 3 = \underline{\hspace{1cm}}$$

Here are twenty-four buttons. If we put the same number of buttons on each of eight cards, how many buttons will we have on each card?

$$8 \times \underline{\hspace{1cm}} = 24$$

or

$$24 \div 8 = \underline{\hspace{1cm}}$$

Here are fifteen cookies. If we put five on a plate, how many plates do we need?

$$\underline{\hspace{1cm}} \times 5 = 15$$

or

$$15 \div 5 = \underline{\hspace{1cm}}$$

Here are fifteen cookies. If we put the same number on each of three plates, how many cookies will be on each plate?

$$3 \times \underline{\hspace{1cm}} = 15$$

or

$$15 \div 3 = \underline{\hspace{1cm}}$$

We can find a missing factor by dividing.

Division

$36 \div 9 = 4 \leftarrow$ quotient

dividend   divisor

$4 \leftarrow$ quotient

$9\overline{)36} \leftarrow$ dividend

divisor

$36 \leftarrow$ dividend

$\dfrac{36}{9} = 4$

divisor

$\leftarrow$ quotient

Each of these is read, "Thirty-six divided by nine equals four."

The multiplication facts will help you remember the division facts.

Give the quotients.

1. $16 \div 4 =$ ___ $\times 4 = 16$

2. $28 \div 4 =$ ___ $\times 4 = 28$

3. $36 \div 6 =$

4. $18 \div 9 =$

5. $25 \div 5 =$

6. $48 \div 8 =$

7. $54 \div 9 =$

8. $42 \div 7 =$

9. $64 \div 8 =$

10. $32 \div 4 =$

___ $\times 7 = 21$

11. $7\overline{)21}$

12. $8\overline{)40}$

13. $6\overline{)18}$

14. $7\overline{)49}$

15. $8\overline{)56}$

16. $3\overline{)24}$

17. $9\overline{)81}$

18. $7\overline{)35}$

19. $4\overline{)36}$

20. $3\overline{)27}$

21. $\dfrac{42}{6} =$ ___ $\times 6 = 42$

22. $\dfrac{63}{9} =$

23. $\dfrac{45}{5} =$

24. $\dfrac{40}{5} =$

25. $\dfrac{8}{2} =$

26. $\dfrac{12}{6} =$

27. $\dfrac{72}{8} =$

28. $\dfrac{18}{3} =$

29. $\dfrac{24}{6} =$

30. $\dfrac{15}{3} =$

Multiplication and division are related

We can write fact teams for multiplication and division facts.

5, 6, 30
5 × 6 = 30   6 × 5 = 30
30 ÷ 6 = 5   30 ÷ 5 = 6

4, 8, 32
4 × 8 = 32   8 × 4 = 32
32 ÷ 8 = 4   32 ÷ 4 = 8

1. Write fact teams for these sets of numbers.

    a. 7, 21, 3   **f.** 4, 8, 2
    b. 18, 3, 6   **g.** 2, 9, 18
    c. 7, 4, 28   **h.** 40, 5, 8
    d. 3, 27, 9   **i.** 42, 6, 7
    e. 5, 7, 35   **j.** 24, 6, 4

2. Give the quotients.

    a. 1 ÷ 1 =
    b. 2 ÷ 1 =
    c. 3 ÷ 1 =
    d. 4 ÷ 1 =
    e. 5 ÷ 1 =
    f. 6 ÷ 1 =
    g. 7 ÷ 1 =
    h. 8 ÷ 1 =
    i. 9 ÷ 1 =
    j. 10 ÷ 1 =

What is always true when a number is divided by 1?

3. Give the quotients.

    a. 1 ÷ 1 =
    b. 2 ÷ 2 =
    c. 3 ÷ 3 =
    d. 4 ÷ 4 =
    e. 5 ÷ 5 =
    f. 6 ÷ 6 =
    g. 7 ÷ 7 =
    h. 8 ÷ 8 =
    i. 9 ÷ 9 =
    j. 10 ÷ 10 =

What is always true when a number is divided by itself?

4. What is the quotient when 0 is divided by a number?

Using division

A fourth grade class made an insect collection. Each student brought in several insects. This chart shows the number of different insects they had in their collection.

Insect group	Number of insects	Number of boxes needed
Straight-winged (grasshopper, roach)	12	
Half-winged (bugs)	15	
Same-winged (locust)	9	
Scale-winged (butterfly, moth)	30	
Shield-winged (beetles)	21	
Two-winged (flies, mosquitoes)	24	
Membrane-winged (bees, wasps, ants)	27	
Other (flea, termite)	18	

They mounted the insects in boxes with three insects in each box.

1. How many boxes were needed for each insect group?

2. How many boxes were needed altogether?

3. Give the quotients.

a. $72 \div 8 =$
b. $56 \div 7 =$
c. $48 \div 8 =$
d. $54 \div 6 =$
e. $81 \div 9 =$
f. $36 \div 4 =$
g. $40 \div 8 =$
h. $42 \div 7 =$
i. $28 \div 4 =$

j. $4\overline{)40}$

k. $5\overline{)35}$

l. $8\overline{)56}$

m. $6\overline{)36}$

n. $\frac{48}{6} =$

o. $\frac{35}{5} =$

p. $\frac{42}{6} =$

q. $\frac{16}{8} =$

Solving problems

Many grocery stores package the fruit and vegetables before putting them out for sale. Bill made this chart to show what he packaged one morning.

Items	total number	number per tray	number of trays used
Potatoes	36	6	
Tomatoes	40		10
Ears of corn	28	4	
Peaches	64		8
Oranges	72		9
Cucumbers	24	3	
Squash	18	2	
Plums	54		9

1. Copy and complete this chart.

2. Write an equation for each problem. Solve.

   a. Bill put five apples in each of eight trays. How many apples did he package?

   b. How many trays would be needed for 45 ears of corn if Bill put five ears on each tray?

   c. There are three pounds of oranges in one bag. How many pounds would there be in nine bags?

   d. There are 42 peaches to be placed on six trays. How many peaches will be on each tray if each has the same number?

   e. Bill put potatoes in bags. If he puts five pounds in each bag, how many bags will be needed for 35 pounds?

   f. Mrs. Tomm bought four trays of tomatoes. There were five tomatoes on each tray. How many tomatoes did she buy?

   g. A box contained 50 pounds of onions. How many bags would be needed to bag these if five pounds were put in each bag?

Finding remainders

Make a drawing to help you find the answers
to the questions.

1. Bill had 15¢. How many gumdrops could he buy? How
many cents would he have left?

2. Tina had 24¢. How many pieces of bubble gum could
she buy? How many cents would she have left?

3. Lisa had 20¢. How many mints could she buy? How
many cents would she have left?

4. Carey had 17¢. How many candy canes could he buy?
How many cents would he have left?

5. Lynn had 32¢. How many lollipops could she buy?
How many cents would she have left?

We call what is left the *remainder*.

You can write division with remainders this way.

$$\begin{array}{r} 5 \\ 6\overline{)32} \\ -30 \\ \hline 2r \end{array}$$

> How many 6s are in 32? There are
> 5, because 5 × 6 = 30.
> How many are left? There are 2,
> because 32 - 30 = 2.

6. Find the answers.

a. $5\overline{)36}$ **b.** $7\overline{)52}$ **c.** $8\overline{)43}$ **d.** $4\overline{)38}$ **e.** $7\overline{)15}$

f. $6\overline{)35}$ **g.** $7\overline{)26}$ **h.** $3\overline{)20}$ **i.** $8\overline{)27}$ **j.** $5\overline{)42}$

Solving problems

1. There are 28 desks in Miss Wall's room. If she puts four desks in each row, how many rows will she make?
2. The class cut out 42 paper leaves of different colors for window decorations. There are six windows. How many leaves will they use for each window if they put the same number of leaves on each one?
3. Miss Wall's class has 15 verses to learn. If they learn three verses each week, how many weeks will it take to learn them?
4. Miss Wall is reading a book to the class. It has 72 pages. If she reads eight pages each day, how many days will it take to read the book?
5. There is a box with 35 gold stars in it. There are two boys and three girls who want to put stars on the art projects they are making. If they share the stars equally, how many stars can each student have?

6. Give the quotients and the remainders.

a. 54 ÷ 7 =	**b.** 65 ÷ 8 =	**c.** 45 ÷ 8 =	**d.** 53 ÷ 8 =
e. 27 ÷ 4 =	**f.** 37 ÷ 7 =	**g.** 75 ÷ 9 =	**h.** 32 ÷ 6 =
i. 80 ÷ 9 =	**j.** 43 ÷ 5 =	**k.** 19 ÷ 2 =	**l.** 44 ÷ 7 =

Pictograph

The students of Faith Christian School were collecting
books of trading stamps to give to a family that was
getting ready to go to the mission field. This graph shows
how many books were collected by each grade.

Kindergarten	📖 📖
Grade 1	📖 📖 📖 📖
Grade 2	📖 📖 📖 📖
Grade 3	📖 📖 📖 📖 📖 📖
Grade 4	📖 📖 📖 📖 📖 📖 📖 📖
Grade 5	📖 📖 📖 📖 📖 📖 📖
Grade 6	📖 📖 📖

📖 = 4 books

This kind of graph is called a **pictograph.** Each picture of
a book represents four books.

1. Which grade collected the most books?
2. Which grade collected the least books?
3. How many books did grade 2 collect? (How many
   books do you think are represented by a half a book?)
4. List the grades. Write how many books were collected
   by each.

The students in the junior high and the high school also
collected books of stamps.

Grade	7	8	9	10	11	12
Number of books	16	12	20	24	18	10

5. Make a pictograph to show the number of books they
   collected. Make one picture represent four books.

1. Make a drawing to illustrate that 4 × 5 = 20.

2. 6 × 8 = 8 × 6 is an example of the ____ principle for multiplication.

3. What does the first factor of a multiplication equation tell you? What does the second factor of a multiplication equation tell you? What does the product tell you?

4. Solve.

   a. 20   **b.** 65   **c.** 38   **d.** 124   **e.** $4.25
      × 4   × 3   × 6   × 4   × 3

5. Give six multiplication facts that have 24 as the product.

6. Write a story problem that would be solved by this equation: 3 × 15 = ____.

7. Write a cross-product multiplication story problem that would be solved by this equation: 2 × 3 = ____.

8. Make a drawing to illustrate that 15 ÷ 3 = 5.

9. What is always true about the quotient when a number is divided by 1? What is always true about the quotient when a number is divided by itself?

10. Give the quotients.
   a. 16 ÷ 8 =
   b. 32 ÷ 4 =
   c. 42 ÷ 6 =   **d.** $7\overline{)56}$ **e.** $6\overline{)54}$ **f.** $\frac{63}{9}$ =   **g.** $\frac{28}{4}$ =

11. Write a story problem that would be solved by this equation: 45 ÷ 5 = ____.

12. Give the quotients and the remainders.

   a.   **b.**   **c.**
      $6\overline{)58}$ $7\overline{)50}$ $6\overline{)39}$

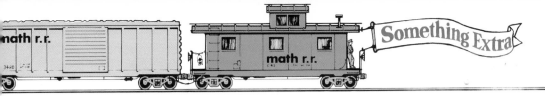
Jerry learned a multiplication trick. It is a way to use his fingers to find the products of multiplication facts that have factors of 6 or greater. Perhaps you would like to try it. This is what you do.

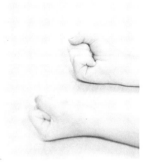

1. Make fists. They each represent the number 5.

2. Represent the numbers 6 through 9 by extending one or more fingers.

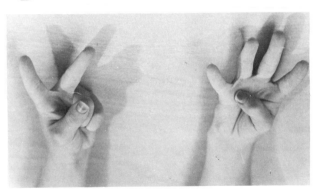

3. Represent a multiplication fact with your hands.
$7 \times 9 = $ ___

4. Add the number of the extended fingers (2 + 4) to find the tens' digit of the product.

5. Multiply the numbers of fingers not extended (3 × 1) to find the ones' digit of the product.
Product: 63

Try some other facts. Do they all work out correctly?
Try $6 \times 6 = $ ___. Can you make it work out?

73

Unit 3

John Henry

John Henry, according to legend, was a worker on the Big Bend railroad tunnel near Hilldale, West Virginia. He probably died in 1872 from overwork. His job was to cut deep holes into the solid rock of the mountain. Into these holes was poured gunpowder which blasted even deeper into the mountain. These holes, when made into railroad tunnels, saved many miles of travel and time for the railroads.

John Henry became a part of American folklore because he worked hard. He did his job better and faster than anyone else. But John Henry did not work hard just to become famous; he worked hard because he had a job he believed was worth doing well.

We may not become famous for doing our jobs well, but it is still our responsibility to do our best. Whether our job is cutting a hole through a mountain or doing math problems, we are responsible to do it as well as we can. (See I Corinthians 10:31.)

Goals for Unit 3

1. I will learn some ways to help myself solve story problems.
2. I will learn how to estimate the cost of two or more items.
3. I will learn how to count out change.
4. I will learn how to read and to make line and bar graphs.
5. I will learn about measuring time.

Words to Remember

estimate	leap year
hour	decade
day	century
week	millennium
month	bar graph
year	line graph

1. Solve these problems.

a. Bob and his parents went camping in Smoky Mountain National Park. They drove 78 miles to the campground, 17 miles while at the campground, and 82 miles to get home. How many miles did they drive altogether?

b. Bob and his father went on a hike each of the four days they camped. It took them three hours to complete each hike. What was the total number of hours they spent hiking?

c. Bob's mother bought peaches for lunch one day. They cost 87¢ for three pounds. What was the cost of one pound of peaches?

d. Bob wanted to buy an Indian headdress that cost $18. He had only $13 to spend. He needed how much more money to buy the headdress?

2. Estimate the costs of these items.

a. 3 pennants at 29¢ each
b. 5 books at 96¢ each

3. Copy and complete.

a. _____ hours = 1 day
b. _____ days = 1 year

4. Bob played Ping-Pong each day with some friends. The graph shows the number of games he won each day.

a. On what day did he win the most games?
b. On what day did he win three games?
c. How many games did he win altogether?

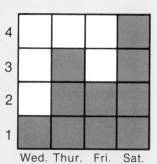

5. What are the coins and bills that would be given as change for these purchases? (Give as few as possible.)

	cost of item	amount given
a.	$0.63	$1.00
b.	1.51	$5.00

77

How To Solve Problems
1. *Read to find the question.*
2. *Read to find the information.*
3. *Decide what to do.*
4. *Figure out the answer.*
5. *Decide if the answer makes sense.*

Do you know when to use each operation?
   Addition
   Subtraction
   Multiplication
   Division

Write *add, subtract, multiply,* or *divide* to tell what you would do if the numbers were given.

1. Melissa had ___ pencils. She gave ___ away. How many did she have left?
2. Oranges cost ___¢ each. Maria bought ___ of them. How much must she pay?
3. A book costs ___¢. Bill has ___¢. How much more does he need to be able to buy the book?
4. Mrs. Smith bought ___ packages of waffles. She bought ___ waffles altogether. How many were in each package?
5. Bob ran ___ miles one week, ___ miles the next week, and ___ the third week. He ran a total of how many miles?
6. Jim learned ___ verses in September, but Trina learned only ___. Jim learned how many more verses than Trina did?

Solving problems

1. Cindy and Troy went to their grandparents' farm. They traveled about 400 miles by plane and 35 miles by car. They traveled about how many miles altogether?

2. Cindy and Troy gathered eggs each morning. During one week they found four dozen eggs. How many eggs did they find?

3. Cindy fed the horses twelve quarts of oats each day. She gave each horse two quarts of oats. How many horses did she feed?

4. Troy liked to help his grandfather pick apples. They picked four baskets of apples one day. Each basket weighed 55 pounds. How many pounds of apples did they pick?

5. Cindy and her grandmother picked corn to sell. They picked 72 ears of corn one morning. How many bags of corn did they have if they put eight ears in a bag?

6. Troy counted six rows of beans in the garden. His grandmother said that each row was 15 meters long. What was the total length of the bean rows?

7. There was a herd of 28 cows on the farm. Nineteen of them were dairy cows and the others were being raised for beef. How many were being raised for beef?

8. Cindy is nine years old. Her grandmother is fifty-three years old. Cindy is how many years younger than her grandmother?

How To Solve Problems
  1. Read to find the question.
  2. Read to find the information.
  3. Decide what to do.
  4. Figure out the answer.
  5. Decide if the answer makes sense.

How can you tell
if an answer is sensible?

Round the numbers to the nearest ten. Then **estimate** the
answer.

1. There are 53 students in the first grade, 48 students in
   the second grade, and 31 students in the third grade.
   There are about how many students in these three
   grades?
2. Brad was counting his seashells. He had 43 mussels,
   36 scallops, 11 conches, and 28 of other kinds. About
   how many seashells did he have altogether?
3. Anna bought nine packages of cookies. There were
   twelve cookies in each package. About how many
   cookies did she buy?
4. Midge had 52¢ but spent 19¢ for a comb. About how
   much did she have left?
5. Benny had 58 rocks to put into boxes. About how
   many boxes would he need if he put nine rocks into
   each box?

Estimating

1. Choose the best estimated cost. (Round to the nearest ten or hundred.)

a. notebook and storybook	$2.00	$3.00	$4.00
b. crayons and pencil	$1.00	$1.50	$2.00
c. ruler and pencil	$0.30	$0.40	$0.50
d. colored paper and pencil	$0.80	$0.90	$1.00
e. ruler and notepad	$0.50	$0.60	$0.70
f. notebook, storybook, and crayons	$3.00	$5.00	$6.00

2. Are these answers sensible? If the answer is no, estimate the answer.

   a. 15 + 38 + 21 + 73 = 147
   b. 37 + 45 + 28 + 62 = 172
   c. 652 + 121 + 847 + 332 = 9,152
   d. 285 + 198 + 413 + 678 = 2,222
   e. 73 - 19 = 92
   f. 82 - 68 = 14
   g. 432 - 198 = 366
   h. 702 - 372 = 330

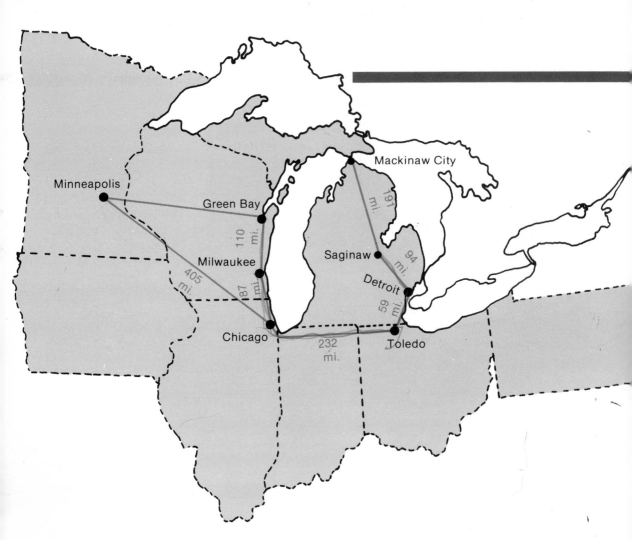

1. Estimate the distance

   a. from Milwaukee to Chicago to Toledo
   b. from Toledo to Detroit to Saginaw
   c. from Green Bay to Milwaukee to Chicago
   d. from Mackinaw City to Saginaw to Detroit

2. Estimate how much

   a. from Chicago to Minneapolis than to Toledo?
   b. from Detroit to Saginaw than to Toledo?
   c. from Toledo to Chicago than to Detroit?
   d. from Milwaukee to Green Bay than to Chicago?
   e. from Saginaw to Mackinaw City than to Detroit?

Making charts

You can make a chart to help you solve problems.

Miss Simms's class had a bake sale to make some money to buy a metric scale for their classroom. The students made charts to help the clerks know how much to charge for each purchase.

1. Complete these charts.

9¢ each
or
2 for 15¢

number of chocolate cookies	2	4	6	8	10	12
cost	15¢					

5¢ each
or
3 for 10¢

number of oatmeal cookies	3	6	9	12	15	18
cost						

10¢ each
or
3 for 25¢

number of brownies	3	6	9	12	15	18
cost						

8¢ each
or
2 for 15¢

number of cupcakes	2	6	10	12	16	20
cost						

2. Find the savings of the special price when buying

    a. 6 brownies
    b. 12 cupcakes
    c. 8 chocolate cookies
    d. 9 oatmeal cookies

Solving problems

Make a chart to help you solve each of these problems.

1. Debby and her father jogged around the ballfield in their neighborhood three evenings each week. Debby went around the ballfield twice in the same amount of time that her father went around it three times. One week Debby jogged around the ballfield twelve times. How many times did her father go around it that week?

Debby						
Father						

2. Mrs. Harris was mixing fertilizer for her plants. The directions said to mix three tablespoons of Speedigrow with four quarts of water. Mrs. Harris planned to use sixteen quarts of water. How many tablespoons of Speedigrow did she use?

Water				
Speedigrow				

3. Danny can ride his bicycle two miles in fifteen minutes. How long will it take him to ride ten miles if he rides at that same speed? (Give the time in minutes.)

Distance					
Time					

4. Sandy practiced the piano thirty minutes each day, but her older brother practiced forty-five minutes each day. If Sandy has practiced 120 minutes so far this week, how many minutes has her brother practiced?

Sandy's time				
Brother's time				

How To Solve Problems
1. Read to find the question.
2. Read to find the information.
3. Decide what to do.
4. Figure out the answer.
5. Decide if the answer makes sense.

Sometimes you must use two or more operations to solve a problem.

1. Gina helped her mother 45 minutes each day after school for five days. She helped her 75 minutes on Saturday. How many minutes did Gina help her mother that week?

2. Jamie had $5.00. He bought a book for $1.35, an ice-cream sandwich for $0.22, and he put $0.75 in the offering at church. How much money did he have left?

3. Mrs. Burt had three dozen eggs. She cooked seven eggs for breakfast. How many eggs did she have left?

4. Freddie weighs 60 pounds; his brother weighs 87 pounds; their father weighs 175 pounds. Freddie and his brother together weigh how much less than their father?

5. Mr. Franz picked 48 pears. He put them in bags with six pears in each bag. He sold them for $0.59 a bag. How much money did he receive?

You can help yourself solve story problems by using one or more of these suggestions.

> **1.** Read it aloud.
> **2.** Draw a picture.
> **3.** Make a chart.
> **4.** Draw a number line.
> **5.** Act it out.

Solve these problems. Use one or more of these suggestions.

1. Jim had five packages of paper that each had 200 sheets. He also had a package that had only 55 sheets left in it. How many sheets of paper did he have altogether?
2. Miss Jones bought a box of cheese crackers for $0.89 and a box of saltines for $0.69. She gave the clerk two dollars. How much change should she receive?
3. Mr. Thomas is twenty inches taller than his son Eric. Eric is 52 inches tall. How tall is Mr. Thomas?
4. Mr. Gray wanted to put a fence around his yard. The yard was square. Each side was 75 feet long. How many feet of fence were needed?
5. Mrs. James baked six dozen cupcakes. She made packages of eight cupcakes to put into the freezer. How many packages could she make?
6. Tonya read three books. Two books had 155 pages each. The other book had 138 pages. How many pages did she read altogether?
7. Miss Clark told her class that if a person ran around the playground nine times, he would have run a mile. Bill and Greg each ran around the playground fifty-four times one week. How many miles did each boy run?
8. Math class started at 10:45 and lasted forty-five minutes. At what time did the class end?

What else do we need to know?

Sometimes we cannot solve problems because they do not give enough information.

Tell what other information is needed to solve these problems.

Tammy and her mother are buying groceries.

1. They bought three packages of frozen corn. What was the total cost of the corn?
2. Tammy wanted to buy ice cream bars. There were twelve bars in each package. How many bars did they buy?
3. The eggs Mrs. Markos bought were $0.72 a dozen. What was the total cost of the eggs?
4. Mrs. Markos paid $0.64 for all the grapefruit she bought. How many grapefruit did she buy?
5. Tammy bought three brownies in the bakery department. They were twenty-two cents each. How much change did she receive?
6. The total cost of the frozen orange juice was $1.80. How many cans did they buy?
7. One tube of toothpaste cost more than another even though they were the same size. How much did Mrs. Markos save by buying the kind that cost $1.09?
8. Tammy chose her favorite soap. It cost $0.59 a bar. What was the total cost of the soap?

Do we need all this information?

Sometimes problems have information that is not needed.

Tell what information about numbers is not needed. Solve each problem.

1. There are thirty students in Mr. Casey's class. Fourteen of them are girls. Mr. Casey formed the class into committees of three students each to work on projects. How many committees did he form?

2. During the month of September Mr. Casey's class collected a total of $24 to send to their class missionary in Brazil. The boys collected $14 and the girls collected $10. The boys collected how much more than the girls?

3. Mr. Casey had a reading contest. The rules said that each book read must have more than fifty pages. Lila read twenty-four books the first week, seventeen books the second week, and twenty-eight books the last week. How many books did Lila read?

4. Eighteen of the students in Mr. Casey's class ride the bus. The rest walk or come by car. Tom rides about fifteen miles on the bus each day. About how many miles does he ride on the bus during one school week?

5. Mr. Casey plans for the class to learn at least twenty-five verses each month for the nine months of school this year. So far they have learned thirty-two verses. How many verses does Mr. Casey plan for his class to learn this year?

Therefore all things whatsoever ye would that men should do to you, do ye even so to them: for this is the law and the prophets.
Matthew 7:12

But God commendeth his love toward us, in that, while we were yet sinners, Christ died for us.
Romans 5:8

Trust in the Lord with all thine heart; and lean not unto thine own understanding. In all thy ways acknowledge him, and he shall direct thy paths.
Proverbs 3:5-6

Can you solve these problems?

Some of these problems have information that is not needed. Others lack necessary information. Solve the problems that you can or tell what information is still needed.

Mrs. Towns and her son Phil live in Philadelphia. They took a trip to Florida.

1. On the first day of travel they drove eight hours. They stopped two times to buy gasoline. It cost $0.32 a liter at the first stop and $0.34 a liter at the second stop. What was the total amount of money they paid for the gasoline they bought that day?

2. Phil chose to eat lunch at McDonald's. The stop took 35 minutes. They bought two cheeseburgers at $0.69 each and two shakes at $0.59 each. How much change did they get from a five-dollar bill?

3. They stayed overnight with Mrs. Towns's sister in Virginia. They arrived there at four o'clock. Phil went to bed at nine o'clock and got up at six o'clock. How many hours was he in bed?

4. Mrs. Towns said that they were traveling about 90 kilometers each hour. It was 400 kilometers to Greenville, South Carolina, where they planned to spend the night. They arrived there at three o'clock. How many kilometers did they travel before lunch?

5. The first stop in Florida was in Jacksonville. They stayed in a motel near the beach. It cost $32 a night. Their evening meal cost $4.95 each. Phil's breakfast cost $1.65 and his mother's cost $1.40. How much did they pay for these meals?

6. The next day they went to Disney World. Mrs. Towns paid $20 for her ticket and $16 for Phil's ticket. How much change did she receive?

7. Mrs. Towns and Phil spent fifteen days away from home altogether. They were in eight states. On the last day they drove about seven hours. They traveled about 80 kilometers each hour. How many kilometers did they travel that day?

1. Find the missing numbers.

	pennies	nickels	dimes	quarters	total value
a.	3	2	6	1	
b.	8	4	0	3	
c.	5	7	4	2	
d.	1	3	7	3	
e.	7	2	4	2	

In the Old Testament God commanded His people to give to Him a *tithe* of everything they received. A tithe meant a tenth. If a man grew 10 ephahs of wheat, he would give one ephah to the Lord. If 100 lambs were born into his flock of sheep, he would give 10 to the Lord. Today, Christians who want to please the Lord give at least a tenth of their income to Him.

> Every man according as he purposeth in his heart, so let him give; not grudgingly, or of necessity: for God loveth a cheerful giver.
>
> II Corinthians 9:7

Income	10¢	$1.00	$10	$100
Tithe	1¢	10¢	$1	$10

2. Use the chart to help you answer these questions.

    a. Tommy earned $2.50 mowing lawns. How much will he give to the Lord?

    b. Mr. Smith's paycheck is $350 each week. How much will he give to the Lord?

    c. Tommy's sister earns $40 each week working after school. How much will she have left after she gives her offering to the Lord?

Making change

Kathy bought a box of crayons for 38¢. She gave the clerk a dollar bill. The clerk gave her two pennies, one dime, and two quarters. Notice the way the clerk counted as she gave the change. Clerks usually give as few coins and bills as possible when they give change to their customers.

38, 39, 40, 50, 75, 1 dollar

1. Count aloud the change that would be given.

	cost of purchase	amount given
a.	$0.33	$0.50
b.	$0.77	$1.00
c.	$1.24	$2.00
d.	$2.67	$3.00
e.	$3.12	$5.00
f.	$4.95	$5.00
g.	$6.78	$10.00

2. Make a chart like this to show what coins would be given in change for the purchases in number 1. Find the total amount of change.

	pennies	nickels	dimes	quarters	dollar bills	total amount of change
a.						
b.						
c.						
d.						
e.						
f.						
g.						

Mrs. Turner checked the prices at three grocery stores before she went shopping for these items. At which store would she pay the least amount of money?

Shopping list:
1 gallon milk
2 cans pineapple
2 dozen eggs
2 packages gelatin
5 pounds potatoes
3 cans tuna fish
1 jar peanut butter
3 heads lettuce
1 cake mix

JOE'S SUPERMARKET

MILK $1.60 with $10.00 order
REGULAR $2.03

pineapple 45¢
eggs 2 doz. for $1.50
gelatin 19¢   potatoes 13¢ A POUND
tuna fish 59¢
peanut butter 99¢
lettuce 39¢
65¢ cake mix

BUY MORE STORE

EGGS 79¢ Per Doz.
MILK - gallon - $2.03
PINEAPPLE 2 for 89¢
GELATIN 3 for 79¢
PEANUT BUTTER $1.06
POTATOES 5 lb. for 69¢
LETTUCE 3 for $1.00
TUNA FISH 65¢
CAKE MIX 59¢

A&B grocery

Milk $1.99
Pineapple 46¢
Eggs 82¢
Gelatin 21¢
Potatoes 12¢ a pound
Tuna Fish 3 for $2.00
Peanut Butter $1.02
Lettuce 37¢
Special Cake Mix 49¢

> And God said, Let there be lights in the firmament of the heaven to divide the day from the night; and let them be for signs, and for seasons, and for days, and for years.
>
> Genesis 1:14

It takes the earth 24 hours to turn around (rotate) one time; therefore there are 24 hours in one day. It takes the earth 365¼ days to travel in an orbit around the sun (revolve); therefore we have 365 days in a year. Every four years we add an extra day to make the extra fourths that we have left out.

> Thus the heavens and the earth were finished, and all the host of them. And on the seventh day God ended his work which he had made; and he rested on the seventh day from all his work which he had made.
>
> Genesis 2:1-2

We have a week of seven days to help us remember that God created the universe in six days and then rested on the seventh day.

> And they lived and reigned with Christ a thousand years.
>
> Revelation 20:4b

When Christ comes back to earth, He will reign as King for one thousand years. We call this thousand years the Millennium. Christians will reign with Him during that time.

> **24 hours = 1 day**
> **7 days = 1 week**
> **365 days = 1 year**
> **366 days = 1 leap year**
> **about 52 weeks = 1 year**
> **12 months = 1 year**
> **10 years = 1 decade**
> **100 years = 1 century**
> **1,000 years = 1 millennium**

1. Complete these charts.

Number of years	1	2	4	6	8
Number of days	365				

Number of years	1	2	3	5	8
Number of weeks	52				

Number of weeks	1	2	4	8	9
Number of days	7				

2. Copy and complete.

    a. 2 weeks 3 days = _____ days
    b. 5 weeks 5 days = _____ days
    c. 2 years 4 months = _____ months
    d. 9 years 3 months = _____ months
    e. 5 years 10 months = _____ months
    f. 18 days = _____ weeks _____ days
    g. 34 days = _____ weeks _____ days
    h. 52 days = _____ weeks _____ days
    i. 60 days = _____ weeks _____ days
    j. 75 days = _____ weeks _____ days

3. How many hours are there in one week?
4. Tina has lived 446 weeks. Is she nine years old?
5. How many months old are you?
6. How many weeks old are you?
7. How many days old are you?

Problems with time

Thirty days hath September,
April, June, and November,
All the rest have thirty-one
Except the second month alone,
To which we twenty-eight assign
Till leap year gives it twenty-nine.

1. April, June, and November have a total of how many days?
2. There are how many weeks and how many days in January?
3. If August 1 is on a Monday, what are the dates of the other Mondays in August?
4. If you borrow a book from the library on October 5 and you may keep it for two weeks, on what date is the book due?
5. What month usually has just four weeks?   February
6. March, May, July, and August have a total of how many days?
7. If today is October 12, what was the date two weeks ago?   What will be the date three weeks from today?
8. How many days are there in three years?
9. How many days are there in four leap years?
10. Jon is nine years old today. How many months old is he? About how many weeks old is he? How many days old is he?

The fourth grade classes in Lake City Christian School made a **bar graph** to show the months of their birthdays.

Months of Our Birthdays

1. Which month has the most birthdays?
2. Which month has the fewest birthdays?
3. What is the total number of birthdays in the first six months of the year?
4. What is the total number of birthdays in the last six months of the year?
5. How many birthdays are represented altogether?
6. Make a birthday graph for your class.

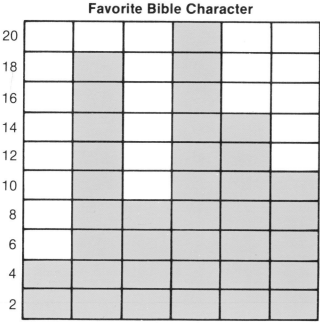

Favorite Bible Character

No. of Children — Joseph Moses Joshua David Samuel Daniel

This bar graph shows the favorite Bible characters of some children.

1. How many children chose David?

2. How many children chose Daniel?

3. How many fewer children chose Joseph than Moses?

4. How many choices are represented on the graph?

5. Solve.

a. 36 $\times$ 4	**b.** 62 $\times$ 6	**c.** 302 - 147	**d.** 614 - 380	**e.** 924 - 397

f. 24 36 + 19	**g.** 84 95 + 39	**h.** 98 74 + 57	**i.** 58 92 + 77	**j.** 39 85 + 78

Line graphs are often used to show how an amount changes over a period of time.

Brad's mother has kept track of Brad's weight from the time he was born. It is shown on this line graph.

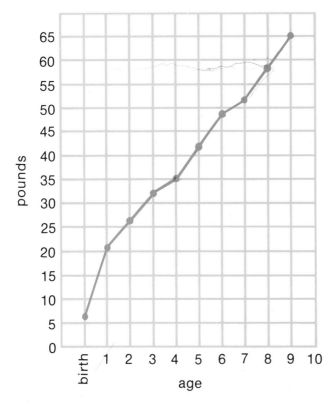

1. Brad gained the most weight during which year?
2. Brad gained the least weight between what ages?
3. How many pounds did Brad gain from birth to age 4?
4. How many pounds did Brad gain from age 4 to age 8?
5. How many pounds did Brad gain from birth to age 9?

Try to find out how much you weighed at birth and on each of your birthdays. Record that information on a line graph.

Temperature on a line graph

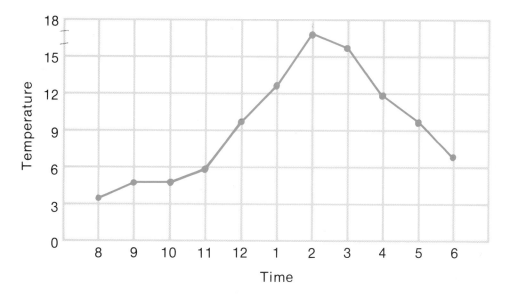

This line graph shows the temperatures on a day in October in Ohio. It uses Celsius degrees.

1. The first temperature is given for what time?
2. The last temperature is given for what time?
3. What was the temperature at noon?
4. What was the temperature at four o'clock?
5. At what time was the temperature highest?
6. How many degrees did the temperature rise between 10 o'clock and 1 o'clock?
7. How many degrees did the temperature fall between 2 o'clock and 6 o'clock?
8. There were how many degrees difference between the highest and the lowest temperatures?

Call the weather bureau and ask for the hourly temperatures. Make a line graph to show these temperatures.

1. Tell what operation is needed to solve each of these problems.

   a. Mr. Collins bought ___ books for his son. If he can put ___ books on a shelf, how many shelves will he need?

   b. Greg needs ___ to pay for a bike that he wants. He has only ___. How much more does he need?

2. Solve.

   a. Bob bought two packages of Ping-Pong balls. Each package cost $1.79. How much change should he receive from five dollars? What coins and bills will he probably receive?

   b. There are twenty-eight students in Miss Cox's classroom. There are sixteen boys and twelve girls. She has formed four teams for a math contest. How many students are on each team?

3. Estimate the cost.

   a. 3 pencils at 19¢ each
   b. 5 books at 95¢ each
   c. 10 Frisbees at $1.89 each

4. Copy and complete.

   a. ___ hours = 1 day
   b. ___ weeks = 1 year
   c. ___ days = 1 year
   d. ___ years = 1 decade
   e. ___ years = 1 century
   f. ___ years = 1 millennium

5. Make a line graph to show Mindy's height from birth to age 5.

Birth	20 in.
1 year	28 in.
2 years	33 in.
3 years	38 in.
4 years	41 in.
5 years	44 in.

Here is a subtraction game to play.

1. Draw a large square and write a number at each corner.
2. Subtract the smaller number from the larger number on each side and write the difference in the middle of that side.
3. Draw another square connecting the differences.
4. Subtract again using the numbers from step 2.
5. Repeat the drawing and subtracting until the differences are all zero.
6. Count the number of squares you have drawn.

      Can you get as many as eight squares?

Here is a completed game. It has five squares.

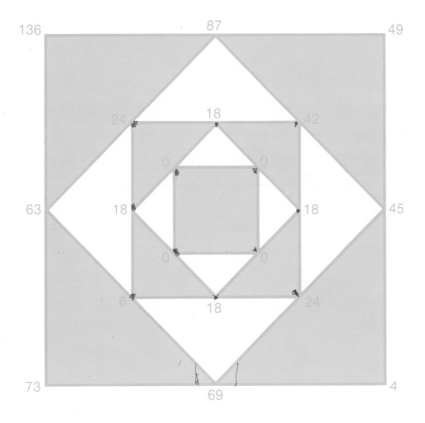

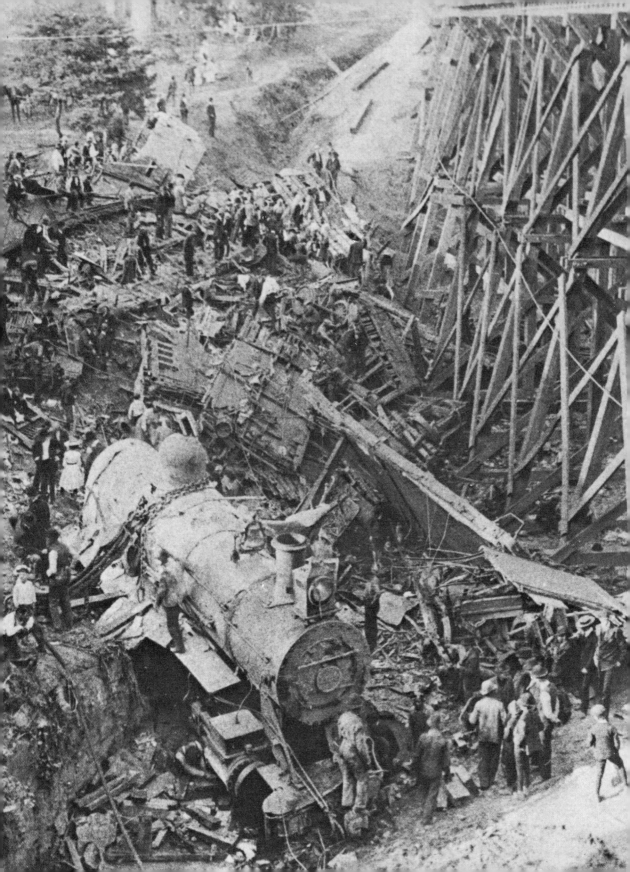

Unit 4

The Wreck of the 97

A person driving a car may resent the law that requires him to stop at a red light. He may feel that no one has a right to tell him how fast he may or may not drive. You may feel that it is unfair of your teacher to require you to be quiet at certain times or to forbid you to play certain games. Usually, however, rules and requirements are for your benefit. The importance of rules is made clear by the story of the accident of the Old 97 on September 27, 1903.

Joe Broady pulled the throttle back. The new engine responded well, picking up speed as it headed into the countryside south of Monroe, Virginia. Joe's responsibility as engineer was to deliver his train of mail to Spencer, and his desire as a good railroader was to be in Spencer on time. As the train rushed out of Monroe, Joe was uneasy because the train had left one hour behind time. He wasn't responsible for the delay, but he was determined to make up the time by running a little faster than usual. Joe was not breaking any rules by running faster on most of the route, but certain sections of track were marked with speed limits. One of these sections included the curve and trestle at Stillhouse Hollow near Danville. Joe saw signs instructing him to slow down as he approached the Hollow, but he knew that if he slowed he could not make it to Spencer on time. He didn't slow down, but neither did he get to Spencer on time. According to the legend, he rounded the curve that led onto the trestle at 90 miles an hour. The engine didn't make the last part of the curve but shot out to the right of the trestle, sailing 100 feet before it smashed into a cow pasture 75 feet below. The impact shattered the cars and they quickly burst into flames. The speed limit had been given for the safety of the train and its crew, but because Joe Broady ignored it, he and twelve other men lost their lives. (See Romans 13:1.)

Goals for Unit 4

1. I will be able to read and write fractions.
2. I will know the renaming principle.
3. I will be able to rename mixed numbers and improper fractions.
4. I will know how to read and write decimal fractions.
5. I will learn how to add and subtract both common and decimal fractions.

Words to Remember

common fraction

numerator

denominator

proper fraction

equivalent

terms

higher terms

lower terms

mixed numbers

improper fraction

decimal

tenths' place

hundredths' place

decimal places

a. b.  c. d.

1. Write the fraction that tells what parts of these figures are colored.

a.  b. c.  d.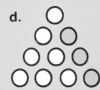

2. Write the fraction that tells what parts of these sets are colored.

3. Write the following in common fraction form and in decimal fraction form:

   a. three-tenths   **b.** one and eight-tenths   **c.** seven-tenths

4. Show these fractions as directed:

   a. Draw a square. Color one-third of it.
   b. Draw a rectangle. Color four-fifths of it.
   c. Draw a circle. Color three-fourths of it.

5. Which is more?

   a. $\frac{3}{5}$ or $\frac{4}{5}$ **b.** $\frac{5}{8}$ or $\frac{7}{8}$ **c.** $\frac{1}{2}$ or $\frac{1}{3}$ **d.** $\frac{1}{4}$ or $\frac{1}{10}$

6. Give equivalent fractions.

7. Write the common fractions that answer these questions.
   a. Jill had three red pencils and four white pencils. What part of her pencils were red?
   b. Mother had six eggs. She cooked five of them. What part of the eggs did she cook?

There are many times when we divide things into equal parts. We use *fractional numbers* to tell about these parts.

The pizza was cut into eight equal parts. Each part is called an *eighth*. Five-eighths of the pizza is in the pan.

The cake was cut into six equal parts. Each part is called a *sixth*. One-sixth of the cake has been taken from the pan.

$\dfrac{5}{8}$ ← These are called **numerators**. → $\dfrac{1}{6}$

These are called **denominators**.

Fractions written in this form are called *common fractions*.

Two equal parts halves	Three equal parts thirds	Four equal parts fourths
		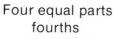

1. Which shows thirds?

2. Which shows fifths?

3. Which shows halves?

a.   b.

a.   b.

a.   b.

c.   d.

c.   d.

c.   d.

For each picture answer these questions.

    a. Into how many equal parts is the figure divided?
    b. What do we call each part?
    c. How many parts are colored?
    d. What part of the whole figure is colored?

1.   2.    3.

4.   5.   6.

7.   8.    9.

10.   11.   12.

When the value of a fractional number is less than one,
we call it a **proper fraction.**

These are proper fractions.   These are not proper fractions.

$\frac{3}{4}$ $\frac{2}{3}$ $\frac{1}{5}$ $\frac{3}{8}$ $\frac{2}{2}$ $\frac{3}{3}$ $\frac{4}{4}$ $\frac{6}{5}$

Sometimes we use fractional numbers to tell about a part of a set.

This box holds eight crayons. Three of the crayons have been taken from the box. Three-eighths of the crayons have been taken from the box.

This carton holds twelve eggs. Seven eggs are in the carton. Seven-twelfths of the eggs are in the carton.

1. What fraction of the pencils *are* is orange?

2. What fraction of the coins *are* is dimes?

3. What fraction of the marbles *are* is orange?

4. What fraction of the eggs *are* is left?

Fractions on a number line

Tom's house   Don's house

Tom has walked $\frac{5}{6}$ of the distance from his house to
Don's house.

Give a fractional number for each colored point on the
number lines.

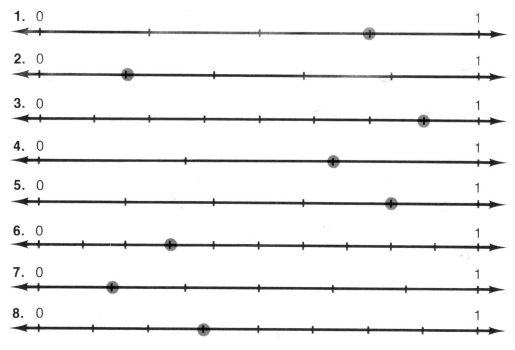

1. 0   1

2. 0   1

3. 0   1

4. 0   1

5. 0   1

6. 0   1

7. 0   1

8. 0   1

Janis folded a sheet of paper into halves. She colored one-half of it red.

$\frac{1}{2}$ is red.

Janis folded the paper again. Then she opened it.

 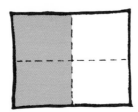

$\frac{2}{4}$ is red.

Can you see that $\frac{1}{2}$ and $\frac{2}{4}$ are names for the same amount of paper?
They are *equivalent fractions*. (The word **equivalent** means "equal value.")

Give equivalent fractions.

1. 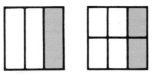 **2.**

3. 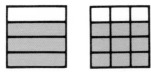 **4.**

5.   **6.**

Terms of a fraction

We call the digits used to write a fractional numeral the **terms** of a fraction. The terms used to write two-thirds are 2 and 3. What are the terms used to write these fractional numerals?

$$\frac{4}{5} \qquad \frac{1}{2} \qquad \frac{3}{10} \qquad \frac{7}{8} \qquad \frac{3}{4}$$

Examine these pairs of equivalent fractions.

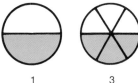 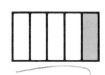 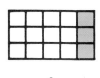

$$\frac{1}{2} = \frac{3}{6} \qquad\qquad \frac{1}{5} = \frac{3}{15}$$

Can you see that the second fraction in each pair has **higher terms** than the first fraction?

Write a pair of equivalent fractions for each picture. Draw a ring around the fraction that has higher terms.

1.   **2.**

3.   **4.**

111

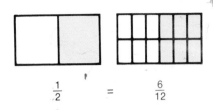

$$\frac{1}{2} = \frac{6}{12}$$

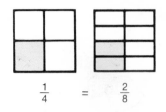

$$\frac{1}{4} = \frac{2}{8}$$

You can find equivalent fractions without drawing pictures.

> Multiply the numerator and denominator of the fraction by the same number (not 0).

$$\frac{6 \times 1}{6 \times 2} = \frac{6}{12} \qquad \frac{2 \times 1}{2 \times 4} = \frac{2}{8}$$

Notice that the equivalent fraction has *higher terms* than the fraction you started with.

1. Find the equivalent fractions.

a. $\dfrac{2 \times 3}{2 \times 4} =$ **b.** $\dfrac{3 \times 1}{3 \times 2} =$ **c.** $\dfrac{2 \times 2}{2 \times 3} =$ **d.** $\dfrac{10 \times 1}{10 \times 2} =$

e. $\dfrac{4 \times 2}{4 \times 5} =$ **f.** $\dfrac{10 \times 5}{10 \times 6} =$ **g.** $\dfrac{5 \times 7}{5 \times 8} =$ **h.** $\dfrac{100 \times 9}{100 \times 10} =$

2. Find five equivalent fractions for each fraction given.

Example: $\dfrac{1}{4}$ $\dfrac{2 \times 1}{2 \times 4} = \dfrac{2}{8}$ $\qquad \dfrac{3 \times 1}{3 \times 4} = \dfrac{3}{12} \qquad \dfrac{4 \times 1}{4 \times 4} = \dfrac{4}{16}$

$\dfrac{5 \times 1}{5 \times 4} = \dfrac{5}{20} \qquad \dfrac{10 \times 1}{10 \times 4} = \dfrac{10}{40}$

a. $\dfrac{1}{2}$ **b.** $\dfrac{2}{3}$ **c.** $\dfrac{1}{6}$ **d.** $\dfrac{3}{4}$

e. $\dfrac{3}{8}$ **f.** $\dfrac{4}{5}$ **g.** $\dfrac{1}{3}$ **h.** $\dfrac{1}{10}$

Renaming fractions using lower terms

There is $\frac{4}{12}$ of a dozen eggs in the carton. We can also say that there is $\frac{1}{3}$ of a dozen eggs in the carton.

$$\frac{4}{12} = \frac{1}{3}$$

Divide both the numerator and denominator of a fraction by the *largest possible* number.

$$\frac{4 \div 4}{12 \div 4} = \frac{1}{3}$$

Examine these other examples.

$$\frac{5 \div 5}{10 \div 5} = \frac{1}{2} \qquad \frac{6 \div 2}{8 \div 2} = \frac{3}{4} \qquad \frac{3 \div 3}{9 \div 3} = \frac{1}{3}$$

Notice that the equivalent fractions have **lower terms.**
Find equivalent fractions that have lower terms.

1. $\frac{10 \div 2}{16 \div 2} =$

2. $\frac{5 \div 5}{25 \div 5} =$

3. $\frac{25 \div 5}{30 \div 5} =$

4. $\frac{8 \div 8}{16 \div 8} =$

5. $\frac{6 \div 3}{9 \div 3} =$

6. $\frac{4 \div 4}{16 \div 4} =$

7. $\frac{9 \div 9}{18 \div 9} =$

8. $\frac{12 \div 2}{14 \div 2} =$

9. $\frac{4 \div 2}{6 \div 2} =$

10. $\frac{9 \div 9}{27 \div 9} =$

11. $\frac{6 \div 6}{18 \div 6} =$

12. $\frac{12 \div 3}{15 \div 3} =$

> Renaming Principle
> The numerator and denominator of a fraction can be multiplied or divided by the same number (not 0) without changing the value of the fraction.

1. Rename these fractions using higher terms.

   a. $\frac{3}{4}$ **b.** $\frac{2}{5}$ **c.** $\frac{1}{8}$ **d.** $\frac{4}{7}$ **e.** $\frac{9}{10}$ **f.** $\frac{2}{3}$

2. Rename these fractions using lower terms.

   a. $\frac{12}{16}$ **b.** $\frac{2}{4}$ **c.** $\frac{9}{12}$ **d.** $\frac{11}{22}$ **e.** $\frac{35}{45}$ **f.** $\frac{7}{14}$

3. Give the missing terms.

   a. $\frac{3}{4} = \frac{}{12}$ **b.** $\frac{5}{8} = \frac{}{16}$ **c.** $\frac{7}{10} = \frac{}{100}$ **d.** $\frac{5}{8} = \frac{}{24}$

   e. $\frac{7}{8} = \frac{14}{}$ **f.** $\frac{3}{4} = \frac{12}{}$ **g.** $\frac{2}{3} = \frac{8}{}$ **h.** $\frac{1}{4} = \frac{4}{}$

4. Give the missing terms.

   a. $\frac{14}{16} = \frac{7}{}$ **b.** $\frac{10}{12} = \frac{5}{}$ **c.** $\frac{4}{8} = \frac{1}{}$ **d.** $\frac{9}{15} = \frac{3}{}$

   e. $\frac{5}{25} = \frac{}{5}$ **f.** $\frac{10}{24} = \frac{}{12}$ **g.** $\frac{6}{20} = \frac{}{10}$ **h.** $\frac{10}{15} = \frac{}{3}$

Cross multiply

$\frac{1}{2}$ ⋈ $\frac{2}{4}$ $1 \times 4 = 4$ Cross
           $2 \times 2 = 4$ multiply.

$\frac{2}{3}$ ⋈ $\frac{4}{6}$ $2 \times 6 = 12$ Cross
           $3 \times 4 = 12$ multiply.

When you cross-multiply a pair of fractions and the products are the same, you know that the fractions are equivalent.

Examine these examples.

$\frac{1}{2} = \frac{3}{6}$ $1 \times 6 = 6$
         $2 \times 3 = 6$

$\frac{2}{3} = \frac{6}{9}$ $2 \times 9 = 18$
         $3 \times 6 = 18$

Copy these pairs of fractions. Cross multiply to see if the fractions are equivalents. Write the sign = or ≠.

Examples: $\frac{3}{5} = \frac{9}{15}$ $3 \times 15 = 45$
                    $5 \times 9 = 45$

$\frac{2}{3} ≠ \frac{9}{12}$ $2 \times 12 = 24$
              $3 \times 9 = 27$

1. $\frac{5}{8}$ ☐ $\frac{3}{4}$

2. $\frac{3}{4}$ ☐ $\frac{9}{12}$

3. $\frac{1}{5}$ ☐ $\frac{5}{25}$

4. $\frac{2}{3}$ ☐ $\frac{8}{15}$

5. $\frac{2}{5}$ ☐ $\frac{8}{25}$

6. $\frac{3}{10}$ ☐ $\frac{15}{50}$

7. $\frac{4}{5}$ ☐ $\frac{9}{12}$

8. $\frac{3}{4}$ ☐ $\frac{9}{15}$

9. $\frac{1}{3}$ ☐ $\frac{5}{15}$

10. $\frac{2}{7}$ ☐ $\frac{5}{14}$

11. $\frac{6}{7}$ ☐ $\frac{12}{20}$

12. $\frac{2}{3}$ ☐ $\frac{8}{12}$

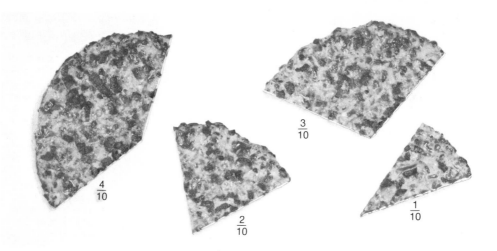

Arrange in order of size from the least to the greatest.
What do you notice about the denominators?
What do you notice about the numerators?

Can you make a rule to follow when comparing fractions
that have denominators that are the same?

Copy and complete. Use > or < . (Example: $\frac{4}{10} > \frac{1}{10}$)

1. $\frac{3}{8}$ □ $\frac{5}{8}$

2. $\frac{3}{5}$ □ $\frac{1}{5}$

3. $\frac{6}{10}$ □ $\frac{9}{10}$

4. $\frac{5}{8}$ □ $\frac{7}{8}$

5. $\frac{2}{3}$ □ $\frac{1}{3}$

6. $\frac{3}{25}$ □ $\frac{1}{25}$

7. $\frac{72}{100}$ □ $\frac{27}{100}$

8. $\frac{19}{50}$ □ $\frac{29}{50}$

9. $\frac{3}{10}$ □ $\frac{1}{10}$

10. $\frac{7}{12}$ □ $\frac{12}{12}$

11. $\frac{1}{100}$ □ $\frac{10}{100}$

12. $\frac{3}{16}$ □ $\frac{10}{16}$

13. $\frac{4}{5}$ □ $\frac{2}{5}$

14. $\frac{3}{20}$ □ $\frac{19}{20}$

15. $\frac{8}{9}$ □ $\frac{7}{9}$

16. Explain in your own words how you know that $\frac{11}{16}$ is greater than $\frac{5}{16}$.

Comparing fractions

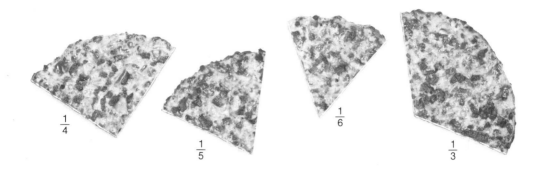

$\frac{1}{4}$

$\frac{1}{5}$

$\frac{1}{6}$

$\frac{1}{3}$

Arrange in order of size from the least to the greatest.
What do you notice about the numerators?
What do you notice about the denominators?

Can you make a rule to follow when comparing fractions
that have numerators that are the same?

Copy and complete. Use $>$ or $<$. (Example: $\frac{1}{6} < \frac{1}{3}$)

1. $\frac{3}{8} \boxdot \frac{3}{10}$

6. $\frac{8}{8} \square \frac{8}{15}$

11. $\frac{5}{5} \square \frac{5}{6}$

2. $\frac{4}{6} \square \frac{4}{15}$

7. $\frac{2}{3} \square \frac{2}{9}$

12. $\frac{15}{28} \square \frac{15}{16}$

3. $\frac{1}{7} \square \frac{1}{8}$

8. $\frac{1}{15} \square \frac{1}{14}$

13. $\frac{1}{9} \square \frac{1}{10}$

4. $\frac{11}{15} \square \frac{11}{12}$

9. $\frac{5}{32} \boxdot \frac{5}{17}$

14. $\frac{4}{5} \square \frac{4}{7}$

5. $\frac{9}{10} \square \frac{9}{20}$

10. $\frac{6}{7} \square \frac{6}{8}$

15. $\frac{3}{11} \square \frac{3}{10}$

16. Explain in your own words how you know that $\frac{2}{3}$ is greater than $\frac{2}{5}$.

Practice

1. Copy and complete. Use = or ≠. (Hint: cross multiply)

a. $\frac{2}{3}$ ☐ $\frac{5}{10}$ b. $\frac{1}{5}$ ☐ $\frac{4}{5}$ c. $\frac{3}{4}$ ☐ $\frac{12}{16}$ d. $\frac{5}{8}$ ☐ $\frac{10}{16}$

e. $\frac{1}{7}$ ☐ $\frac{2}{14}$ f. $\frac{3}{10}$ ☐ $\frac{3}{8}$ g. $\frac{6}{8}$ ☐ $\frac{2}{3}$ h. $\frac{7}{21}$ ☐ $\frac{1}{3}$

i. $\frac{10}{20}$ ☐ $\frac{4}{8}$ j. $\frac{3}{5}$ ☐ $\frac{4}{5}$ k. $\frac{1}{2}$ ☐ $\frac{2}{3}$ l. $\frac{5}{6}$ ☐ $\frac{10}{12}$

2. Copy and complete. Use > or <

a. $\frac{3}{8}$ ☐ $\frac{4}{8}$ b. $\frac{2}{5}$ ☐ $\frac{2}{3}$ c. $\frac{4}{10}$ ☐ $\frac{1}{10}$ d. $\frac{7}{18}$ ☐ $\frac{17}{18}$

e. $\frac{3}{8}$ ☐ $\frac{3}{5}$ f. $\frac{9}{10}$ ☐ $\frac{4}{10}$ g. $\frac{3}{7}$ ☐ $\frac{6}{7}$ h. $\frac{4}{5}$ ☐ $\frac{4}{11}$

i. $\frac{2}{15}$ ☐ $\frac{2}{5}$ j. $\frac{10}{20}$ ☐ $\frac{15}{20}$ k. $\frac{1}{5}$ ☐ $\frac{1}{8}$ l. $\frac{2}{7}$ ☐ $\frac{2}{3}$

3. Copy and complete.

a. $\frac{2}{3} = \frac{4}{}$ b. $\frac{1}{5} = \frac{}{10}$ c. $\frac{3}{8} = \frac{9}{}$ d. $\frac{1}{10} = \frac{}{30}$ e. $\frac{7}{8} = \frac{}{24}$

f. $\frac{3}{4} > \frac{}{4}$ g. $\frac{6}{15} > \frac{6}{}$ h. $\frac{1}{2} > \frac{1}{}$ i. $\frac{2}{3} > \frac{}{3}$ j. $\frac{5}{8} > \frac{5}{}$

k. $\frac{1}{5} < \frac{1}{}$ l. $\frac{2}{5} < \frac{}{5}$ m. $\frac{7}{10} < \frac{7}{}$ n. $\frac{10}{30} < \frac{}{30}$ o. $\frac{9}{10} = \frac{}{10}$

Mixed numeral and improper fractions

These pies were left after dinner. There were $2\frac{1}{3}$ pies left.

We can say that there were $\frac{7}{3}$ pies left.

Give a mixed number and an improper fraction for each picture.

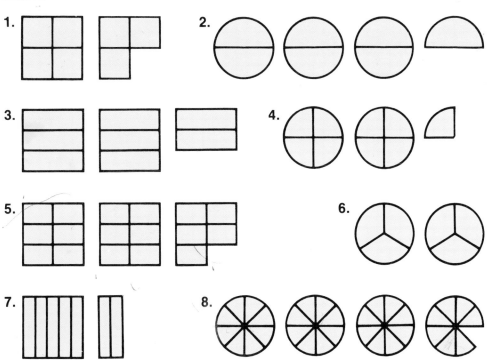

1.

2.

3.

4.

5.

6.

7.

8.

Renaming mixed numerals

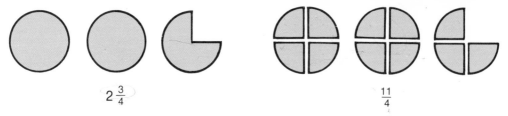

$2\frac{3}{4}$ $\frac{11}{4}$

We can rename mixed numbers as improper fractions without using pictures.

Think: **1.** How many fourths in one whole? *four fourths*

      2. How many fourths in two wholes? *eight fourths*

      3. 8 fourths and 3 fourths are how many fourths? *11 fourths*

Copy and complete.

1. $3\frac{1}{3} = \frac{}{3}$ **5.** $5\frac{1}{8} = \frac{}{8}$ **9.** $4\frac{3}{5} = \frac{}{5}$

2. $1\frac{7}{8} = \frac{}{8}$ **6.** $3 = \frac{}{4}$ **10.** $7\frac{1}{2} = \frac{}{2}$

3. $4\frac{1}{2} = \frac{}{2}$ **7.** $2\frac{4}{5} = \frac{}{5}$ **11.** $8 = \frac{}{3}$

4. $2\frac{1}{5} = \frac{}{5}$ **8.** $3\frac{9}{10} = \frac{}{10}$ **12.** $5\frac{1}{3} = \frac{}{3}$

Renaming improper fractions

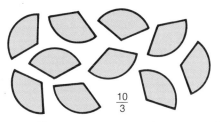

$\frac{10}{3}$

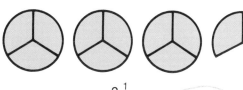

$3\frac{1}{3}$

You can rename improper fractions as mixed numbers or whole numbers without pictures.

Think: **1.** How many thirds make 1 whole? (3 thirds)

2. How many sets of 3 thirds in 10 thirds? (3 sets)

3. How many thirds are left? (1 third)

Rename these improper fractions as whole numbers or mixed numbers.

1. $\frac{7}{5}$　　**2.** $\frac{11}{4}$　　**3.** $\frac{8}{3}$　　**4.** $\frac{12}{5}$　　**5.** $\frac{18}{2}$　　**6.** $\frac{14}{5}$

7. $\frac{25}{4}$　　**8.** $\frac{30}{7}$　　**9.** $\frac{15}{2}$　　**10.** $\frac{12}{4}$　　**11.** $\frac{61}{10}$　　**12.** $\frac{18}{5}$

13. $\frac{63}{9}$　　**14.** $\frac{32}{5}$　　**15.** $\frac{41}{6}$　　**16.** $\frac{18}{3}$　　**17.** $\frac{21}{4}$　　**18.** $\frac{17}{2}$

Practice

1. Copy and complete.

   a. $1\frac{1}{5} = \frac{}{5}$ **b.** $3\frac{1}{4} = \frac{}{4}$ **c.** $2\frac{1}{8} = \frac{}{8}$ **d.** $7\frac{1}{3} = \frac{}{3}$ **e.** $2\frac{3}{5} = \frac{13}{}$

   f. $2\frac{3}{4} = \frac{}{4}$ **g.** $3\frac{5}{8} = \frac{29}{}$ **h.** $5\frac{1}{6} = \frac{}{6}$ **i.** $6\frac{1}{10} = \frac{}{10}$ **j.** $4\frac{2}{3} = \frac{14}{}$

2. Rename each improper fraction as a whole number or a mixed number.

   a. $\frac{17}{4}$ **b.** $\frac{30}{5}$ **c.** $\frac{16}{7}$ **d.** $\frac{22}{5}$ **e.** $\frac{15}{8}$ **f.** $\frac{35}{3}$

   g. $\frac{64}{9}$ **h.** $\frac{55}{6}$ **i.** $\frac{27}{4}$ **j.** $\frac{71}{9}$ **k.** $\frac{85}{9}$ **l.** $\frac{100}{10}$

3. Arrange these numbers into four columns:

Whole numbers	Mixed numbers	Improper fractions	Proper fractions

   $\frac{3}{4}$ $\frac{15}{3}$ 7 $\frac{8}{8}$ $2\frac{1}{6}$ $\frac{17}{4}$ 9 $\frac{5}{8}$ $\frac{31}{7}$

   $5\frac{2}{3}$ $\frac{9}{10}$ $\frac{75}{5}$ 23 $3\frac{1}{5}$ $6\frac{2}{7}$ $\frac{22}{3}$ $\frac{8}{9}$ $\frac{9}{10}$

4. Copy and complete. Use $=$ and $\neq$.

   a. $\frac{5}{8} \square \frac{10}{16}$ **b.** $\frac{3}{4} \square \frac{12}{15}$ **c.** $\frac{3}{6} \square \frac{1}{3}$ **d.** $\frac{7}{14} \square \frac{1}{2}$ **e.** $\frac{3}{15} \square \frac{1}{5}$

   f. $\frac{4}{5} \square \frac{2}{3}$ **g.** $\frac{2}{5} \square \frac{10}{25}$ **h.** $\frac{6}{18} \square \frac{1}{3}$ **i.** $\frac{4}{16} \square \frac{1}{4}$ **j.** $\frac{6}{30} \square \frac{1}{5}$

   k. $\frac{3}{7} \square \frac{1}{3}$ **l.** $\frac{3}{10} \square \frac{8}{50}$ **m.** $\frac{2}{9} \square \frac{6}{45}$ **n.** $\frac{4}{12} \square \frac{1}{3}$

Adding and subtracting fractions

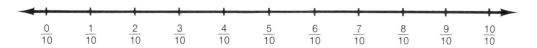

$$\frac{0}{10} \quad \frac{1}{10} \quad \frac{2}{10} \quad \frac{3}{10} \quad \frac{4}{10} \quad \frac{5}{10} \quad \frac{6}{10} \quad \frac{7}{10} \quad \frac{8}{10} \quad \frac{9}{10} \quad \frac{10}{10}$$

Use the number line to help you find the answers to these problems.

Amy walked $\frac{2}{10}$ of a mile then ran for $\frac{1}{10}$ of a mile. How far had she gone?

Tom ran $\frac{4}{10}$ of a mile. Jim ran $\frac{7}{10}$ of a mile. Jim ran what part of a mile farther than Tom?

   2 tenths
  + 1 tenth $\frac{2}{10} + \frac{1}{10} = \frac{3}{10}$
   3 tenths

   7 tenths
  - 4 tenths $\frac{7}{10} - \frac{4}{10} = \frac{3}{10}$
   3 tenths

Solve. Give the answers in the lowest terms.

1. $\frac{3}{5} + \frac{1}{5} =$ **7.** $\frac{11}{12} - \frac{7}{12} =$

2. $\frac{1}{3} + \frac{1}{3} =$ **8.** $\frac{9}{10} - \frac{3}{10} =$

3. $\frac{7}{10} + \frac{1}{10} =$ **9.** $\frac{5}{6} - \frac{1}{6} =$

4. $\frac{3}{7} + \frac{1}{7} =$ **10.** $\frac{3}{4} - \frac{1}{4} =$

5. $\frac{2}{5} + \frac{2}{5} =$ **11.** $\frac{5}{8} - \frac{3}{8} =$

6. $\frac{3}{8} + \frac{3}{8} =$ **12.** $\frac{7}{10} - \frac{1}{10} =$

Practice adding and subtracting fractions

$\frac{3}{5} + \frac{3}{5} = \frac{6}{5} = 1\frac{1}{5}$

$\frac{5}{9} + \frac{7}{9} = \frac{12}{9} = 1\frac{3}{9} = 1\frac{1}{3}$

Solve. Rename answers when necessary.

1. $\frac{3}{8} + \frac{5}{8} =$

6. $\frac{1}{4} + \frac{1}{4} + \frac{3}{4} =$

2. $\frac{9}{10} + \frac{3}{10} =$

7. $\frac{5}{8} + \frac{1}{8} + \frac{7}{8} =$

3. $\frac{2}{3} + \frac{2}{3} =$

8. $\frac{3}{10} + \frac{7}{10} + \frac{9}{10} =$

4. $\frac{4}{5} + \frac{3}{5} =$

9. $\frac{1}{9} + \frac{7}{9} + \frac{1}{9} =$

5. $\frac{4}{7} + \frac{6}{7} =$

10. $\frac{5}{6} + \frac{5}{6} + \frac{5}{6} =$

Solve.

1. Kim ran $\frac{3}{4}$ of a mile and then she walked $\frac{3}{4}$ of a mile. How far did she go altogether?

2. Mrs. Nelson had $\frac{3}{4}$ pound of butter. She used $\frac{1}{4}$ pound in her cookies. How much butter did she have left?

3. Mrs. Nelson made a large pizza and cut it into eight equal pieces. Mr. Nelson ate $\frac{3}{8}$ of the pizza, Mike ate $\frac{3}{8}$ of it, and Kim ate the rest. What part of the pizza did Kim eat?

4. Jeff practiced piano for $\frac{2}{3}$ of an hour. Then he spent $\frac{1}{3}$ of an hour doing his homework. How long did he spend on this work?

5. Mrs. Nelson bought $\frac{3}{4}$ pound of sliced ham, $\frac{1}{4}$ pound of salami, and $\frac{3}{4}$ pound of bologna. How much meat did she buy altogether?

Practice

1. Make drawings to show the following:
   a. three-fourths of a square
   b. one-sixth of a circle
   c. two-thirds of a rectangle.

2. Tell what part of each drawing is colored.

a.   **b.**   **c.**   **d.**   **e.**   **f.**

3. Give an equivalent fraction in higher terms.
   a. $\frac{3}{4}$ **b.** $\frac{2}{5}$ **c.** $\frac{1}{12}$ **d.** $\frac{2}{3}$ **e.** $\frac{5}{8}$

4. Give an equivalent fraction in lower terms.
   a. $\frac{10}{20}$ **b.** $\frac{6}{8}$ **c.** $\frac{8}{12}$ **d.** $\frac{5}{15}$ **e.** $\frac{35}{45}$

5. Copy and complete. Use =, >, or <.
   a. $\frac{3}{4} \square \frac{6}{8}$ **b.** $\frac{5}{8} \square \frac{5}{9}$ **c.** $\frac{1}{3} \square \frac{1}{2}$ **d.** $\frac{2}{10} \square \frac{1}{5}$

6. Copy and complete.
   a. $2\frac{1}{3} = \frac{}{3}$ **b.** $3\frac{4}{5} = \frac{}{5}$ **c.** $2\frac{1}{8} = \frac{}{8}$ **d.** $6\frac{2}{5} = \frac{}{5}$

7. Rename each improper fraction as a whole number or a mixed number.
   a. $\frac{14}{5}$ **b.** $\frac{22}{7}$ **c.** $\frac{17}{4}$ **d.** $\frac{23}{6}$ **e.** $\frac{11}{3}$

8. Solve. Give the answers in lowest terms.
   a. $\frac{1}{8} + \frac{3}{8} =$ **b.** $\frac{3}{5} + \frac{4}{5} =$ **c.** $\frac{1}{3} + \frac{1}{3} =$ **d.** $\frac{5}{8} + \frac{5}{8} =$

   e. $\frac{3}{10} + \frac{7}{10} =$ **f.** $\frac{11}{12} - \frac{5}{12} =$ **g.** $\frac{7}{8} - \frac{3}{8} =$ **h.** $\frac{7}{9} - \frac{2}{9} =$

Fractions in decimal form

Jeff has an odometer on his bicycle. It measures the distance he rides.
Picture A shows the odometer when he has ridden seven-tenths of a mile.
Picture B shows it when he has ridden ten-tenths or one whole mile.

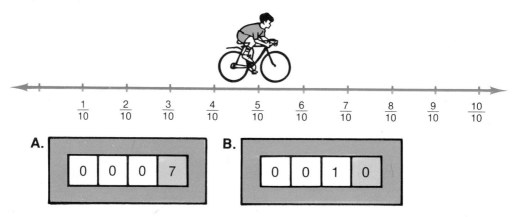

How many miles are shown on these odometers? Read aloud.

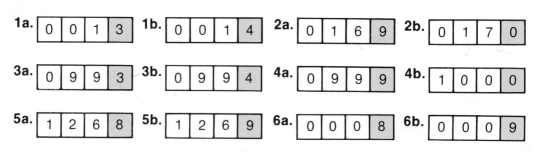

1a. 0 0 1 3 **1b.** 0 0 1 4 **2a.** 0 1 6 9 **2b.** 0 1 7 0

3a. 0 9 9 3 **3b.** 0 9 9 4 **4a.** 0 9 9 9 **4b.** 1 0 0 0

5a. 1 2 6 8 **5b.** 1 2 6 9 **6a.** 0 0 0 8 **6b.** 0 0 0 9

The white part of the dial on the odometer shows the whole numbers and the colored part shows the tenths.

When fractional numbers and mixed numbers are written in *decimal form,* they look something like the dial of an odometer. A dot called a **decimal** is written between the ones' place and the **tenths' place**.

7. Read aloud.

    a. 0.7   **b.** 3.5   **c.** 7.8   **d.** 25.3   **e.** 50.2

Tenths

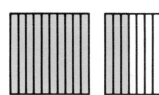

$1\frac{3}{10}$

common fraction form

ones	tenths
1	3

table form

1.3

decimal fraction form

1. Read these sentences aloud.

   a. Mr. Long's car can travel about 18.6 miles on one gallon of gas.
   b. Mary's temperature was 101.8 degrees when she was sick.
   c. The pencil weighs 2.3 grams.
   d. Chris ran 0.9 mile without stopping.
   e. The giraffe is 3.9 meters tall.

2. How much is colored? Write your answer in both common fraction form and decimal fraction form.

a.
b.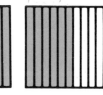

c.  d.

3. Write in decimal form.

   a. five and six-tenths
   b. three and four-tenths
   c. two and one-tenth
   d. six-tenths
   e. one and nine-tenths

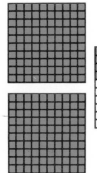 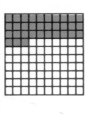

$2\frac{33}{100}$

common
fraction
form

ones	tenths	hundredths
2	3	3

table form

2.33

decimal
fraction
form

1. How much is colored? Give your answers in both common fraction and decimal form.

a.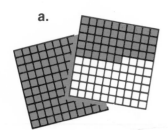

b.

c.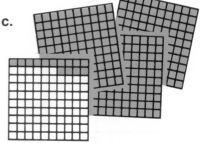

hundreds	tens	ones	tenths	hundredths
1	3	6	2	5

136.25

2. Examine the chart that shows place values.

   a. What is the value of the place in the center?

   b. What is the value of the place just left of the ones' place?

   c. What is the value of the place just right of the ones' place?

   d. What is the value of the place that is two to the left of the ones' place?

   e. What is the value of the place that is two to the right of the ones' place?

The decimal *points* to the ones' place. When we know which is the ones' place, it is easy to remember the value of the other places.

Decimal place value

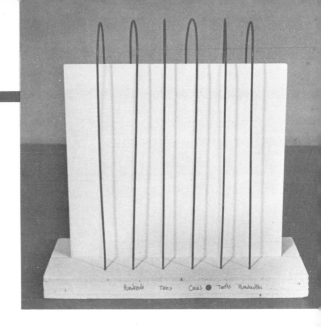

The abacus can help us understand the decimal form of writing fractions.

1. How many ones equal one ten?
2. How many tens equal one hundred?
3. How many tenths equal one whole?
4. How many hundredths equal one tenth?

The places to the right of the ones' place are called **decimal places.**

These charts show some world records for running and swimming. They were the records in 1978. Some of them may have been broken since then. Read the times aloud.

Records for Swimming 100 Meters				
	Men		Women	
Stroke	minutes	seconds	minutes	seconds
Free-style	0	49.44	0	55.41
Breast	1	2.86	1	10.31
Butterfly	0	54.18	0	59.46
Back	0	55.49	1	1.51

Records for Running				
	Men		Women	
Event	minutes	seconds	minutes	seconds
100 meters		9.95		10.88
200 meters		19.83		22.06
400 meters		43.86		49.02
800 meters	1	43.4	1	54.9
1,500 meters	3	32.2	3	56.0

129

Adding and subtracting decimal fractions

Miss Jones bought 16.5 liters of gasoline on Monday and 18.4 liters on Saturday. How many liters of gasoline did she buy that week?

$$16.5 + 18.4 =$$

Add the tenths.	Add the whole numbers.	Write the decimal to show which is the ones' place.
16.5 + 18.4 9	16.5 + 18.4 34 9	16.5 + 18.4 34.9

The gas tank of Mr. Reeves's van holds 78.8 liters of gasoline. His Volkswagen holds only 40.1 liters. The van holds how many more liters of gasoline than the Volkswagen?

$$78.8 - 40.1 =$$

Subract the tenths.	Subtract the whole numbers.	Write the decimal to show which is the ones' place.
78.8 - 40.1 7	78.8 -40.1 38 7	78.8 - 40.1 38.7

Solve.

1. 39.3 + 56.4 =
2. 74.8 + 25.1 =
3. 27.2 + 63.7 =
4. 34.1 + 62.5 =
5. 92.4 + 14.3 =
6. 54.3 + 36.3 + 14.2 =
7. 11.5 + 26.1 + 82.3 =

8. 42.2 + 36.3 + 15.4 =
9. 36.2 + 35.1 + 62.3 =
10. 93.1 + 36.5 + 82.2 =
11. 85.6 - 24.1 =
12. 72.5 - 38.4 =
13. 46.8 - 29.3 =
14. 90.9 - 36.5 =

15. 25.7 - 18.2 =
16. 89.9 - 26.6 =
17. 34.6 - 28.2 =
18. 56.5 - 37.2 =
19. 95.8 - 46.7 =
20. 73.9 - 29.6 =

Addition with renaming

4.76 + 8.49 =

Add the hundredths. Rename as tenths and hundredths.	Add the tenths. Rename as ones and tenths.	Add the whole numbers.	Write the decimal to show which is the ones' place.
׀ ׀ 4.76 + 8.49 5	׀ ׀ 4.76 + 8.49 25	׀ ׀ 4.76 + 8.49 13 25	׀ ׀ 4.76 + 8.49 13.25

Explain how to solve these problems.

2.38 + 1.79 4.17	5.63 + 2.92 8.55	9.18 + 2.25 11.43

Solve.

1. 82.36 + 14.95 =
2. 24.59 + 61.14 =
3. 8.26 + 7.52 =
4. 14.82 + 9.78 =
5. 1.91 + 63.45 =

6. 2.89 + 3.54 + 6.95 =
7. 5.36 + 2.94 + 8.61 =
8. 2.69 + 5.82 + 0.77 =
9. 0.82 + 0.75 + 0.26 =
10. 5.36 + 0.65 + 1.24 =

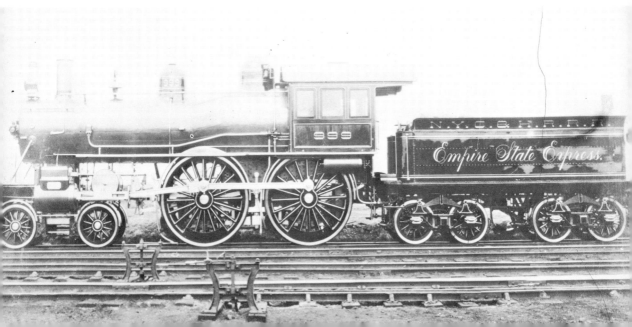

Subtraction with renaming

6.31 - 3.58 =

Rename a tenth as hundredths. Subtract the hundredths.	Rename a one as tenths. Subtract the tenths.	Subtract the whole numbers.	Write the decimal to show which is the ones' place.
$\overset{2\ 11}{6.3\cancel{1}}$ $-\ 3.58$ 3	$\overset{5\ \overset{12}{\cancel{2}}\ 11}{6.3\cancel{1}}$ $-\ 3.58$ 73	$\overset{5\ \overset{12}{\cancel{2}}\ 11}{6.3\cancel{1}}$ $-\ 3.58$ 2 73	6.31 $-\ 3.58$ 2.73

Explain how to solve these problems.

5.42	3.38	7.01
- 1.68	- 1.19	- 2.73

Solve.

1. 4.38 - 1.54 =
2. 8.14 - 3.75 =
3. 7.52 - 1.99 =
4. 5.64 - 2.39 =
5. 7.18 - 4.05 =

6. 9.26 - 1.77 =
7. 3.33 - 1.58 =
8. 2.64 - 0.87 =
9. 3.02 - 1.36 =
10. 7.11 - 2.58 =

Extra practice

1. 6.24 + 3.52 =
2. 8.75 + 1.98 =
3. 2.68 + 7.46 =
4. 3.65 + 3.65 =
5. 7.95 + 3.87 =
6. 4.76 + 5.95 =
7. 2.38 + 7.87 =
8. 6.73 + 4.88 =
9. 9.08 + 3.87 =
10. 8.76 + 0.95 =

11. 8.64 - 6.25 =
12. 4.05 - 1.23 =
13. 7.56 - 3.29 =
14. 14.00 - 6.08 =
15. 10.32 - 7.82 =
16. 24.16 - 11.19 =
17. 35.07 - 15.86 =
18. 24.11 - 16.37 =
19. 73.45 - 26.28 =
20. 16.01 - 9.83 =

Find the distances
1. from the White House to the Capitol.
2. from Union Station to the Smithsonian Institution.
3. from the Lincoln Memorial to Ford's Theater.
4. from the Jefferson Memorial to the Washington Memorial to the Lincoln Memorial.
5. from the Smithsonian Institution to the Museum of Natural History to the National Gallery of Art.

1. Write the decimal form of the number shown on each abacus.
2. How many hundredths are needed to equal one-tenth?
3. How many tenths are needed to equal one whole?
4. Write the following in decimal form.
   a. sixteen and five-tenths
   b. thirty-five hundredths
   c. four and seven-hundredths
   d. twenty and fifty-eight hundredths
   e. one and six-tenths
5. Solve.
   a. 4.2 + 1.8 =
   b. 7.14 + 2.36 =
   c. 1.82 + 6.47 =
   d. 5.29 + 3.08 + 0.17 =
   e. 0.63 + 19.54 + 3.76 =
6. Solve.
   a. 8.6 - 3.4 =
   b. 5.0 - 2.8 =
   c. 26.14 - 13.32 =
   d. 17.02 - 8.45 =
   e. 30.14 - 12.62 =

7. Weight in kilograms

Mr. Greaves	78.6
Mrs. Greaves	50.3
Paul	63.7
Ginger	40
Tim	32.6
Melissa	8.4

a. Paul weighs how much more than his mother?
b. How much do Paul and Tim weigh together?
c. What is the combined weight of Ginger and Melissa?
d. Mrs. Greaves weighs how much less than her husband?
e. What is the total weight of the Greaves family?

Early settlers of our country often used the wild plants they found growing all about them as some of their main sources of food. The common cattail can be made into many delicious dishes.

The pollen of the cattail can be used to make pancakes. Collect the pollen from the heads of ripe cattails. Bend the head of the cattail over an open container or bag. Shake the pollen off or rub it off with your hand. Sift the pollen before using it in your pancakes.

$\frac{3}{4}$ cup flour	1 cup water
$\frac{3}{4}$ cup cattail pollen	1 beaten egg
3 teaspoons baking powder	$\frac{1}{8}$ cup salad oil
$\frac{1}{3}$ cup powdered milk	$\frac{1}{8}$ teaspoon salt

Mix the flour, powdered milk, pollen, and baking powder in a bowl. In another bowl mix the water, egg, salad oil, and salt. Add the liquid mixture to the dry ingredients. Stir only until the dry ingredients are moistened. The batter will be lumpy.

Pour the batter onto a hot griddle. Bake until the top is bubbly and the bottom side is golden brown. Turn the pancake to cook on the other side.

Unit 5

Kate Shelley

On the evening of July 6, 1881, fifteen-year-old Kate Shelley and her mother listened to a thunderstorm rage around their Iowa home. Kate had been checking on the farm animals all evening, afraid that the little pigs would drown or the other animals would wander too close to the fast-flowing river. At 11:00 P.M. they heard the whistle of a locomotive checking the bridges for washouts. They heard the engine cross the Des Moines River bridge and approach the little bridge over Honey Creek. The crash that followed left no doubt about what had happened to the engine.

The two women knew that the men in the engine needed help and that the Midnight Limited would soon come racing down that same track if someone didn't do something. Kate took her father's railroad lantern and started out the door. Her mother prayed for her safety and told her, "Go, . . . do what you can!" Kate ran to the Honey Creek bridge. The men were safe and did not need her help. She thought of the Midnight Limited, which would soon follow this engine into the river if it were not stopped.

In the rain she ran west toward the village of Moingona to stop the train, but between her and the village lay the Des Moines River, by now a raging torrent carrying bridges and trees that it had ripped from its banks. As Kate approached the railroad bridge, she stumbled and fell, breaking her lantern. Now the darkness was broken only by jagged streaks of lightning. Kate started crawling across the shaking railroad bridge. The rough wood and sharp nails tore her skin and clothes. Great trees missed her by inches as they were swept under the bridge. The pounding rain blinded her and made it hard for her to keep her balance. Finally, Kate made it across the bridge and to the village where she was able to stop the train.

Kate Shelley did what needed doing. She did not wait to be told; she did not give the responsibility to someone else. Kate saved more than 200 lives and became an American railroad legend because she did what she could. (See Colossians 3:23.)

Goals for Unit 5

1. I will know and be able to use units of measure in the metric system.
2. I will know and be able to use units of measure in the customary system.
3. I will learn to read the scale on a map or drawing.
4. I will be able to locate a point on a grid.
5. I will learn how the years are counted.

Words to Remember

meter	milliliter
decimeter	inch
centimeter	foot
millimeter	yard
kilometer	mile
perimeter	cup
polygon	pint
regular polygon	quart
triangle	half-gallon
square	gallon
pentagon	ounce
hexagon	pound
heptagon	ton
octagon	scale drawing
gram	grid
kilogram	Before Christ (B.C.)
liter	Anno Domini (A.D.)

What do you remember?

1. Measure. Give the length in centimeters.

   a. _____

   b. _____

   c. _____

2. Measure. Give the length in inches.

   a. _____

   b. _____

   c. _____

3. Copy and complete.

   a. 1 pound = _____ ounces

   b. 1 foot = _____ inches

   c. 1 quart = _____ pints

   d. 1 yard = _____ feet

   e. 1 meter = _____ centimeters

   f. 1 kilogram = _____ grams

   g. 1 liter = _____ milliliters

   h. 1 kilometer = _____ meters

   i. 1 mile = _____ feet

   j. 1 yard = _____ inches

   k. 1 gallon = _____ quarts

   l. 1 pint = _____ ounces

4. Which is more?

   a. 1 quart or 3 pints

   b. 2 pounds or 40 ounces

   c. 3 yards or 6 feet

   d. 100 centimeters or 1 kilometer

   e. 5 feet or 2 yards

   f. 48 inches or 5 feet

1 meter = 10 decimeters (dm)
1 meter = 100 centimeters (cm)
1 meter = 1,000 millimeters (mm)
1,000 meters = 1 kilometer (km)

Most people in the world measure distance with these standard units. These are units of the *metric system.*

1. Find three things in your classroom that are about 1 meter long.
2. Find a place on your body that is about 1 meter from the floor.
3. Measure the length and width of your classroom in meters.
4. Is the distance across the palm of your hand more than, less than, or about the same as 1 decimeter?
5. Draw a line segment that is about 1 decimeter long.
6. Measure the width of each of the fingers on one hand. Are any of them about 1 centimeter wide?
7. Estimate the length of this line segment. Measure it to see how close your estimate is.

────────────────────

8. Try to find a place that is 1 kilometer from the school. You can probably walk 1 kilometer in about 10 minutes.

Complete this chart. Each column measures the same length.

meters	1	2	5			15
decimeters	10	20			100	
centimeters	100		500			
millimeters	1,000			9,000		

Practice

1. Fill in each blank with one of these units of measure:
   kilometer, meter, decimeter, centimeter, millimeter.

   a. Mr. Smith is almost 2 ___ tall.
   b. Bill's shoe was about 20 ___ long.
   c. Mindy lives 4 ___ from the school.
   d. The Bible is about 4 ___ thick.
   e. The truck is almost 10 ___ long.
   f. It is about 5,000 ___ from Florida to California.
   g. The sheet of cardboard was about 2 ___ thick.

2. Estimate the lengths. Measure to the nearest centimeter.

   a. _____
   b. _____
   c. _____

3. Copy and complete.

   a. 5 meters = ___ centimeters
   b. 20 centimeters = ___ decimeters
   c. 50 kilometers = ___ meters
   d. 3 centimeters = ___ millimeters
   e. 10 decimeters = ___ centimeters

4. Draw line segments that you think are these lengths. Then measure to
   find out how close you were.

   a. 7 cm   **b.** 6 mm   **c.** 2 dm   **d.** 12 cm   **e.** 40 mm

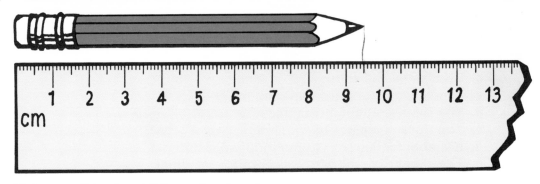

This pencil is about 9.5 centimeters long.

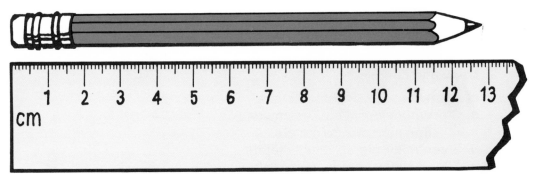

This pencil is about 12.8 centimeters long.

1. Measure to the nearest tenth of a centimeter.

    a. _____

    b. _____

    c. _____

    d. _____

    e. _____

2. Draw line segments that are these lengths.

    a. 5.5 centimeters

    b. 8.2 centimeters

    c. 15 centimeters

    d. 12.8 centimeters

    e. 8.7 centimeters

1. Craig received a dog for his birthday. He and his father plan to put a fence around part of their backyard for the dog. This drawing shows the size of the yard they will enclose. How many meters of fence must they buy?

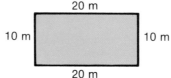

2. Find the distance around these figures.

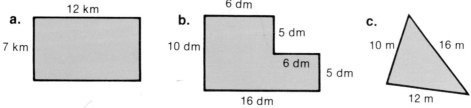

a. 35 cm, 15 cm, 30 cm

b. 8 m, 8 m, 8 m, 8 m

c. 7 m, 16 m, 13 m

The word **perimeter** means "the distance around."

3. Find the perimeter of these figures.

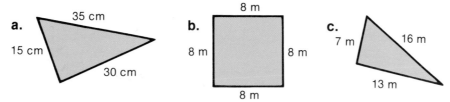

a. 12 km, 7 km

b. 6 dm, 5 dm, 10 dm, 6 dm, 5 dm, 16 dm

c. 10 m, 16 m, 12 m

4. The book of Exodus records the story of the building of the Tabernacle. God told Moses how the Tabernacle was to be built.

   a. What is the perimeter of the Outer Court?

   b. What is the perimeter of the Holy Place?

   c. What is the perimeter of the Holy of Holies?

   d. Find the perimeters using metric measure.

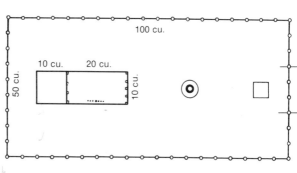

143

Adding and subtracting measures

It is easy to add and subtract measurements.

```
   3 m 61 cm
 + 5 m 23 cm
   8 m 84 cm
```

```
  15 m 45 cm
 - 8 m 23 cm
   7 m 22 cm
```

Solve.

1.   5 cm 2 mm
     + 8 cm 4 mm

2.   17 m 3 dm
     + 28 m 6 dm

3.   2 m 4 dm
       + 8 m 5 dm

4.   7 dm 8 cm
     - 2 dm 1 cm

5.   25 m 9 dm
     - 18 m 9 dm

6.   15 cm 6 mm
       - 9 cm 2 mm

Sometimes you must change one unit of measure to another.

```
   1
   6 cm 5 mm
 + 2 cm 8 mm
   9 cm 3 mm
```
Rename 13 mm as 1 cm and 3 mm.

```
   7  11
   8 cm 1 mm
 - 6 cm 8 mm
   1 cm 3 mm
```
Rename 1 cm as 10 mm.

7.   3 m 8 dm
     + 1 m 7 dm

8.   7 cm 8 mm
     + 1 cm 6 mm

9.   5 m 4 dm
       + 2 m 8 dm

10.   6 m 2 dm
      - 1 m 8 dm

11.   16 cm 4 mm
       - 5 cm 6 mm

12.   8 dm
       - 3 dm 5 cm

Finding perimeters

Figures with three or more sides are called **polygons.** The sides of **regular polygons** are the same length. You can multiply to find the perimeter of regular polygons.

Polygons

Number of sides	Name of figure
3	triangle
4	square
5	pentagon
6	hexagon
7	heptagon
8	octagon

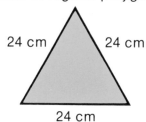

24 cm   24 cm

24 cm

$$\begin{array}{r} 24 \\ \times\ 3 \\ \hline 72 \end{array}$$

The perimeter of the triangle is 72 centimeters.

1. Find the perimeter of each regular polygon.

a.

38 dm

d.

72 m

b.
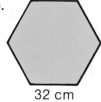
32 cm

e.

17 mm

c.

216 m

f.
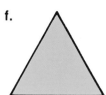
175 m

2. Multiply.

a. 7 × 69 =

b. 9 × 314 =

c. 2 × 920 =

d. 8 × 37 =

e. 7 × 123 =

f. 6 × 50 =

g. 3 × 275 =

h. 6 × 87 =

i. 4 × 132 =

j. 5 × 79 =

The metric units of weight that are most often used are the gram and the kilogram.

1,000 grams = 1 kilogram (kg)

A jellybean weighs about 1 gram.

This book weighs about 1 kilogram.

1. Which unit should be used—gram or kilogram?

a. 2 _____   **b.** 10 _____   **c.** 2 _____

d. 280 _____   **e.** 15 _____

2. Collect five objects. Estimate their weights. Weigh each object. Record your information on a chart like this one.

Object	Estimated weight	Measured weight

Measuring capacity with the metric system

The metric units of capacity that are most often used are the liter and the milliliter.

1 liter = 1,000 milliliters (ml)

This cola bottle holds 1 liter.

A milliliter is the same as a few drops.

A teaspoon holds about 5 milliliters.

A cup holds about 250 milliliters.

1. Collect five jars. Arrange them according to how much you think they hold. Measure to find their capacities. Did you have them in the right order?

2. Solve.
   a. One paper cup holds 190 milliliters. How much will five paper cups hold?
   b. One pail holds 12 liters. How many liters will nine pails hold?
   c. One gasoline tank holds 65 liters. How many liters will six tanks hold?
   d. One jar holds 315 milliliters. How many milliliters will four jars hold?
   e. One bathtub holds 400 liters. How many liters will eight bathtubs hold?

1 foot = 12 inches
1 yard = 36 inches
1 yard = 3 feet
1 mile = 5,280 feet
1 mile = 1,760 yards

1. Name three things that are about one inch long.
2. Name three things that are about one foot long.
3. Name three things that are about one yard long.
4. Try to find a place that is about one mile from your home. About how long do you think it would take to walk one mile?
5. Complete these charts.

a.

feet	1	2	3	4	5
inches	12				

b.

yards	1	2	3	4	5
inches	36				

c.

yards	1	2	3	4	5
feet	3				

6. Copy and complete. Use >, <, or =.

a. 3 ft. ☐ 30 in.
b. 12 ft. ☐ 5 yd.
c. 100 in. ☐ 9 ft.
d. 50 in. ☐ 2 yd.
e. 32 ft. ☐ 10 yd.

f. 20 in. ☐ 3 ft.
g. 72 in. ☐ 6 ft.
h. 7 yd. ☐ 20 ft.
i. 5 ft. ☐ 60 in.
j. 9 yd. ☐ 25 ft.

Inches

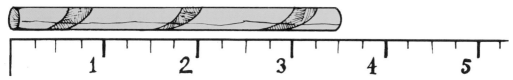

This straw is about $3\frac{1}{2}$ inches long.

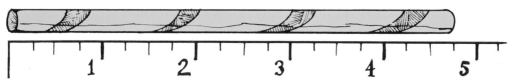

This straw is about $4\frac{3}{4}$ inches long.

1. Measure.

   a. _____

   b. _____

   c. _____

   d. _____

   e. _____

2. Draw line segments that are these lengths.

   a. $3\frac{1}{4}$ inches

   b. $6\frac{1}{2}$ inches

   c. $2\frac{3}{4}$ inches

   d. $1\frac{1}{2}$ inches

   e. $5\frac{1}{4}$ inches

Practice

1. Copy and complete.

a. 6 ft. 5 in. = _____ in.　　　f. 7 yd. 1 ft. = _____ ft.

b. 7 ft. 2 in. = _____ in.　　　g. 1 yd. 7 in. = _____ in.

c. 12 ft. 6 in. = _____ in.　　　h. 2 yd. 20 in. = _____ in.

d. 3 yd. 2 ft. = _____ ft.　　　i. 4 yd. 15 in. = _____ in.

e. 6 yd. 1 ft. = _____ ft.　　　j. 10 yd. 10 in. = _____ in.

2. Solve.

a.　　3 ft. 6 in.　　b.　14 ft. 8 in.　　c.　　7 ft. 5 in.　　d.　　9 ft.
　　+ 5 ft. 2 in.　　　+ 38 ft. 2 in.　　　+ 12 ft. 4 in.　　　+ 6 ft. 5 in.

e.　42 ft. 9 in.　　f.　73 ft. 5 in.　　g.　100 ft. 7 in.　　h.　68 ft. 9 in.
　- 18 ft. 6 in.　　　- 26 ft. 3 in.　　　- 78 ft. 4 in.　　　- 19 ft. 2 in.

Remember to change from one unit to another if necessary.

```
    1
  3 ft. 8 in.     Rename 14 in. as
+ 4 ft. 6 in.     1 ft. 2 in.
  8 ft. 2 in.
```

```
  5  15
  6 ft. 3 in.     Rename 1 ft. as
- 1 ft. 9 in.     12 in.
  4 ft. 6 in.
```

i.　　7 ft. 9 in.　　j. 15 ft. 10 in.　　k.　72 ft. 8 in.　　l.　32 ft. 9 in.
　+ 2 ft. 6 in.　　　+ 13 ft.　8 in.　　　+ 36 ft. 5 in.　　　+ 66 ft. 5 in.

m.　9 ft.　4 in.　　n. 11 ft. 7 in.　　o.　106 ft.　　　p.　30 ft. 1 in.
　- 5 ft. 10 in.　　　- 5 ft. 9 in.　　　- 28 ft. 2 in.　　　- 18 ft. 6 in.

Usual lengths of train cars

Freight train		Passenger train	
Box car	40 ft. 6 in.	Baggage car	65 ft.
Flat car	53 ft. 7 in.	Express car	81 ft.
Hopper	40 ft.	Diner	82 ft.
Stock car	44 ft.	Sleeping car	78 ft.
Tank car	45 ft.	Passenger coach	69 ft.

1. What is the total length of a box car, a flat car, and a tank car?
2. What is the length of five hoppers?
3. A flat car is how much longer than a box car?
4. What is the length of six tank cars?
5. A diner is how much longer than a passenger coach?
6. What is the length of eight passenger coaches?
7. An express car is how much longer than a baggage car?
8. What is the total length of a baggage car, a diner, two sleeping cars, and five passenger cars?

2 cups (c.) = 1 pint (pt.)
2 pints = 1 quart (qt.)
2 quarts = 1 half-gallon
4 quarts = 1 gallon (gal.)

1. Copy and complete.

a. 2 gal. = _____ qt.

b. 6 qt. = _____ pt.

c. 10 pt. = _____ c.

d. 5 gal. = _____ qt.

e. 4 pt. = _____ c.

f. 6 pt. = _____ qt.

g. 8 qt. = _____ gal.

h. 10 c. = _____ pt.

i. 12 qt. = _____ gal.

j. 18 pt. = _____ qt.

2. Solve.

a. Mrs. Smith bought four half-gallons of milk. This was the same amount as how many quarts of milk?

b. Ed has a quart jar full of acorns. How many pint jars could he fill with those acorns?

c. The cook prepared two gallons of orange drink. How many pitchers could be filled if each pitcher holds one quart?

d. Mother made twelve quarts of punch for a party. How many gallon jars would this fill?

e. The glasses in the lunchroom hold one cup each. How many glasses can be filled with one gallon of water?

Pounds and ounces

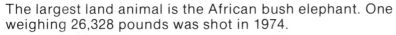

16 ounces (oz.) = 1 pound (lb.)
2,000 pounds = 1 ton (T.)

The abbreviation for pound (lb.) comes from the Latin word *libra*, which means pound.

A female blue whale may weigh as much as 200 tons. This is 400,000 pounds.

The largest land animal is the African bush elephant. One weighing 26,328 pounds was shot in 1974.

The smallest mammal is the bumblebee bat. An adult weighs between 0.06 and 0.07 ounces.

The largest deer is the Alaskan moose, which may weigh as much as one ton. The smallest deer is the pudu of South America. The adult weighs from 18 to 20 pounds.

The largest marsupial (pouched animal) is the red kangaroo. It may weigh 175 pounds. The marsupial mouse weighs only about 0.14 ounces.

A St. Bernard named Duke weighed 295 pounds. An adult Yorkshire terrier named Sylvia weighed only 10 ounces.

Copy and complete.

1. 3 pounds = _____ ounces
2. 5 pounds = _____ ounces
3. 9 pounds = _____ ounces
4. 3 tons = _____ pounds
5. 5 tons = _____ pounds

6. 1 pound 6 ounces = _____ ounces
7. 2 pounds 10 ounces = _____ ounces
8. 3 pounds 1 ounce = _____ ounces
9. 3 tons 100 pounds = _____ pounds
10. 8 tons 1,450 pounds = _____ pounds

Metric System of Measure   ## Customary System of Measure

grams
kilograms

liters
milliliters

inches
feet
yards
miles

cups
pints
quarts
gallons

meters
kilometers
centimeters
millimeters

pounds
ounces
tons

Nearly all the countries of the world use the metric units for measuring. Here in the United States we use the units from both systems. Some like the metric system better; some prefer the customary system.

Complete each chart.

Meters	1	2	3	6	8
Centimeters					
Kilograms	1	3	5	7	9
Grams					
Liters	1	2	4	8	9
Milliliters					

Yards	1	2	3	6	8
Inches					
Pounds	1	3	5	7	9
Ounces					
Quarts	1	2	4	8	9
Cups					

Which charts were easier to complete?

1 bath = about 8 gallons
1 cubit = about 18 inches
1 firkin = about 9 gallons
1 hin = about 6 pints
1 homer = about 86 gallons
1 span = about 9 inches

Use your Bible and this chart to help you answer the following questions.

1. Goliath was about how many inches tall? (I Samuel 17:4)
2. About how many gallons did each waterpot hold? (John 2:6)
3. How many pints of oil were used for the meat offering? (Numbers 15:9)
4. How many gallons did each laver in Solomon's temple hold? (I Kings 7:38)
5. How many gallons did the molten sea in Solomon's temple hold? (II Chronicles 4:2a, 5b)
6. How tall was the image that Nebuchadnezzar built? (Daniel 3:1)
7. How much barley seed could be bought for fifty shekels of silver? (Leviticus 27:16b)

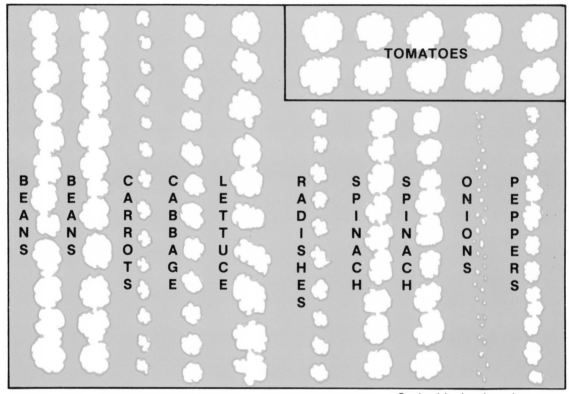

Scale: 1 inch = 1 yard

This is a **scale drawing** of a garden.
Use your ruler to find the answers to these questions.

1. How many yards long is the garden?
2. How many yards wide is the garden?
3. What is the total length of the rows of beans?
4. What is the perimeter of the part of the garden that is used for the tomatoes?
5. What is the total length of the rows of spinach?
6. What is the perimeter of the garden in yards?
7. What is the perimeter of the garden in feet?

156

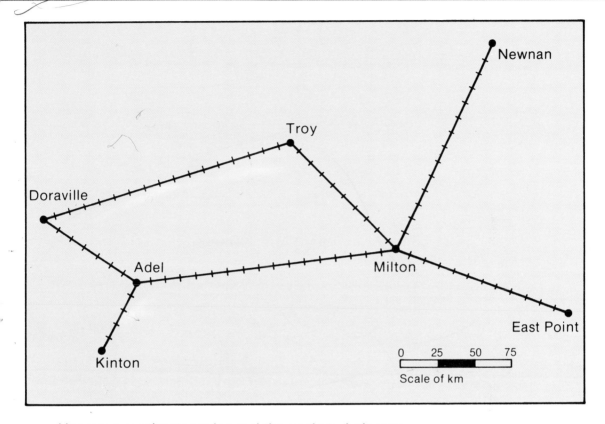

Use your centimeter ruler and the scale to help you complete this chart that shows the distances by railroad.

From	To	number of centimeters on map	number of kilometers
Doraville	Adel		
East Point	Milton		
Adel	Kinton		
Troy	Doraville		
East Point	Doraville		
Newnan	Doraville		

157

Locating points

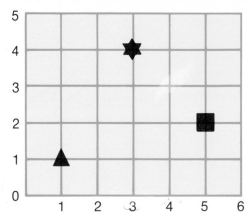

Mrs. Hadik told her class that they could give the location of the star on the **grid** with the number pair (3,4). Can you explain what she meant?

The class figured out that they must start at 0, go to the right 3 units, then go up 4 units.

What number pair gives the location of the triangle? What number pair gives the location of the square?

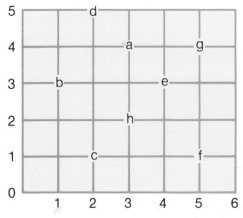

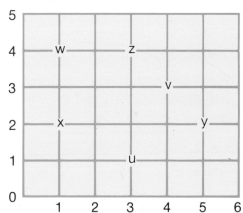

1. Complete each number pair.

a (3,)	e (4,)
b (1,)	f (5,)
c (2,)	g (,4)
d (2,)	h (,2)

2. Give the number pair for each letter.

z	w
y	v
x	u

A message

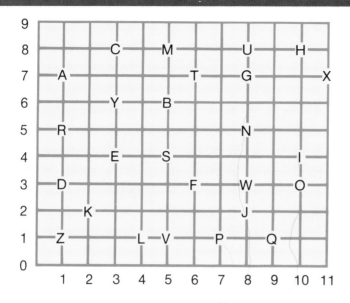

Find the message.

(6,7) (10,8) (3,4)   (6,3) (3,4) (1,7) (1,5)   (10,3) (6,3)   (6,7) (10,8) (3,4)

(4,1) (10,3) (1,5) (1,3)   (10,4) (5,4)   (6,7) (10,8) (3,4)

(5,6) (3,4) (8,7) (10,4) (8,5) (8,5) (10,4) (8,5) (8,7)   (10,3) (6,3)

(2,2) (8,5) (10,3) (8,3) (4,1) (3,4) (1,3) (8,7) (3,4)

Your teacher will give you the reference for this verse.
Find it in the Bible and copy the rest of the verse.

What does the Lord call a person who despises
wisdom and instruction?

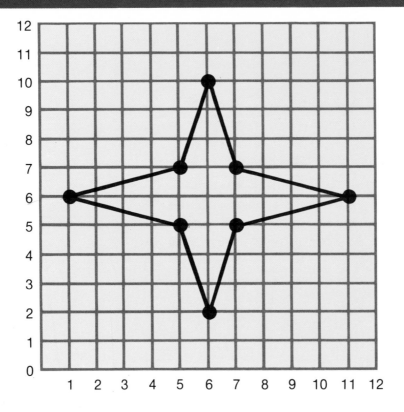

This design was made by locating and then connecting these points in order.
Start (1,6)→(5,5)→(6,2)→(7,5)→(11,6)→(7,7)→
(6,10)→(5,7)→(1,6)→End

Make a picture by connecting these points in order.
(Your teacher will give you the paper to use.)

Start(5,1)→(9,1)→(9,3)→(11,10)→(9,12)→(5,12)→(3,10)→
(5,3)→(5,1)
Start(7,4)→(8,4)→(8,5)→(9,5)→(9,6)→(8,6)→(8,9)→(7,9)→
(5,6)→(5,5)→(7,5)→(7,4)
Start(6,6)→(7,6)→(7,7)

Time lines

Important events in our lives help us to keep track of time. The most important event of all time was Christ's coming to earth to die for our sins and provide salvation for us. We should be reminded of that event every time we write the date.

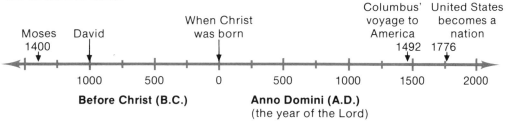

1. About how many years were there from the time of Moses until the time of David?
2. About how many years were there from the time of David until the time of Christ?
3. About how many years were there from the time of Christ until Columbus came to America?
4. About how many years are there from the time of Christ until now?
5. How many years are there from the time the United States became a nation until now?
6. About how many years are there from the time of Moses until now?

161

Railroad history

1810   1820   1830   1840

1830 first train in United States

1814 first train with cars   first sleeping car 1837

The dates below the line tell when the railroad first opened for business in these countries.

1825 Great Britain   1832 France   1837 Russia

1830 United States

1. The first train with cars was built in England in 1814. How many years went by before the first train was used in the United States?
2. How many years have trains been used in the United States?
3. The first dining car was built how many years after the first sleeping car?
4. The first air-conditioned train was built how many years after the first dining car?
5. The first train in the United States traveled about 36 miles per hour. How many years went by before a train could travel 100 miles per hour?

1870   1880   1890   1900

trains carried 79 billion tons per mile 1890   1893 first train to go 100 m.p.h.

1872 Japan   1883 China   1891 Palestine

162

Railroad history

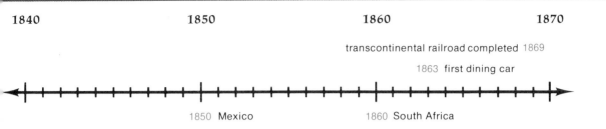

1840   1850   1860   1870

transcontinental railroad completed 1869

1863 first dining car

1850 Mexico   1860 South Africa

6. How much more were the railroads carrying in 1916 than in 1890?
7. Great Britain used the railroad how many years earlier than the United States?
8. China's first railroad began how many years after the first railroad in the United States?
9. Which country's first railroad began in 1850? This was how many years after the first railroad in France?
10. In what year was Palestine's first railroad begun? This was how many years ago?
11. Which country began to use the railroad 42 years after the United States did?

1900   1910   1920   1930

trains carried 366 billion tons per mile 1916   first air-conditioned train 1931

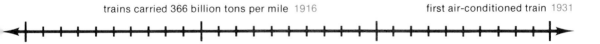

1. Copy and complete.

    a. _____ centimeters = 1 meter

    b. _____ grams = 1 kilogram

    c. _____ millimeters = 1 centimeter

2. Copy and complete.

    a. _____ inches = 1 foot

    b. _____ ounces = 1 pound

    c. _____ quarts = 1 gallon

3. Mrs. Hall has a garden in the shape of a square. Each side is 20 feet in length. What is the perimeter of the garden?

4. Miss Henson made 12 quarts of tea. How many one-gallon pitchers would it fill?

5. Marie is 4 feet 3 inches tall. How many inches tall is she?

6. Mr. Brown was born in 1940. How old was he in 1975?

7. Find the message.

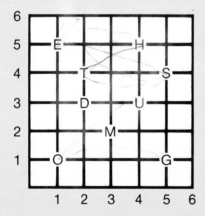

(2,4) (4,5) (1,1) (4,3) (5,1) (1,1) (2,3)

(5,4) (1,5) (1,5) (5,4) (2,4) (3,2) (1,5)

8.

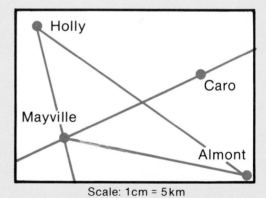

Scale: 1cm = 5km

    a. What is the distance from Mayville to Caro?

    b. What is the distance from Almont to Holly?

    c. What is the distance from Almont to Mayville?

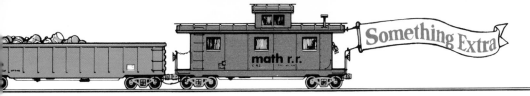

Can you imagine changing your watch twenty times as you took a train trip from Maine to California? This was necessary until 1883 when a group of railroad men decided to form time zones. These time zones were such a good idea that in 1918 Congress established the standard time zones as the legal way of determining time throughout the United States.

This map shows the standard time zones of the United States. Notice that the hours are earlier as you go toward the west and later as you go toward the east.

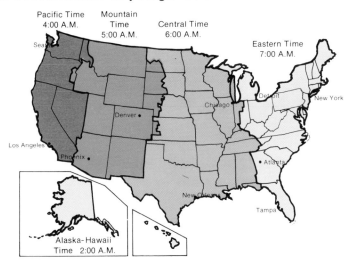

Pacific Time
4:00 A.M.

Mountain Time
5:00 A.M.

Central Time
6:00 A.M.

Eastern Time
7:00 A.M.

Seattle

Denver

Los Angeles

Phoenix

Chicago

Detroit

New York

Atlanta

New Orleans

Tampa

Alaska-Hawaii Time 2:00 A.M.

1. It is 8 o'clock in Denver. What time is it in Chicago?
2. It is 4 o'clock in Atlanta. What time is it in New Orleans?
3. It is 1 o'clock in Los Angeles. What time is it in Denver?
4. It is 6 o'clock in Phoenix. What time is it in Atlanta?
5. It is 10 o'clock in New York. What time is it in Seattle?
6. It is 12 o'clock noon in Detroit. What time is it in Hawaii?
7. What time zone do you live in? What time is it now? What time is it in Tampa?

Unit 6

Engine No. 999

In 1893 the owners of the New York Central Railroad decided that they were going to have the fastest train in the world. They designed Engine Number 999 with the idea of making it the fastest engine yet.

On its first trip on May 10, 1893, a short three-car train carrying several officials and timekeepers started on a specially cleared section of track. The engineer let out the throttle slowly as they passed through some small towns and up some low hills until he reached a thirty-six mile stretch of track that was perfectly level and straight. The time had come. The engineer pulled the throttle back as far as it could go. In the passenger car the officials became white with fear. They had been expecting a fast ride, but this was incredible. The timekeepers glanced at their watches and at one another. They were the first to realize that Number 999 had just made history. It had broken all speed records by reaching a speed of 112.5 miles per hour. Nothing on wheels had ever gone so fast before. Engine Number 999 was immediately world famous. It was put on display at the Chicago World's Fair. Its fame, however, did not last long.

The great 999 could not pull any normal load. It was very fast but, as engines go, it was weak. Several times in the next few years it was modified and adapted in an effort to make it a stronger locomotive. Every effort failed. It is good for an engine to be fast, but it is more important that it be able to pull a heavy load. Many times Christians give all their energy and time to strive for a goal that may be good, but in reaching that goal they sacrifice the things that are really important. Anytime we do too much of a good thing and forget part of God's will for us, we are sinning. (See I Timothy 4:8.)

Goals for Unit 6

1. I will learn how to factor numbers.
2. I will learn the grouping principle for multiplication.
3. I will be able to multiply and divide with large numbers.

Words to Remember
factor
multiple
common multiple
grouping principle

1. Solve.

   a. 3 × 38 =   **b.** 7 × 245 =   **c.** 8 × $3.62 =

2. Solve.

   a.   **b.**   **c.**   **d.**   **e.**

    9)40   7)59   4)38   3)25   6)52

3. Give three multiplication facts with a product of 24.

4. Give three multiplication facts with a product of 36.

5. Give two multiplication facts with a product of 18.

6. Copy and complete. Use the multiplication-addition principle.

   a.   5 × 35   **b.**   6 × 48   **c.**   9 × 26

    (5 × 30) + (5 × _)   (_ × 40) + (_ × 8)   (_ × _) + (_ × _)

    ___ + ___   ___ + ___   ___ + ___

    ___   ___   ___

7. Write a story problem for each of these equations.

   a. 7 × $5.25 = _____

   b. 85 ÷ 9 = _____

8. Give the products.   **9.** Give the quotients.

   a. 7 × 9 =   **a.** 35 ÷ 5 =

   b. 8 × 6 =   **b.** 18 ÷ 3 =

   c. 5 × 9 =   **c.** 27 ÷ 9 =

   d. 9 × 8 =   **d.** 56 ÷ 7 =

   e. 6 × 9 =   **e.** 63 ÷ 9 =

   f. 7 × 4 =   **f.** 49 ÷ 7 =

   g. 8 × 7 =   **g.** 42 ÷ 6 =

   h. 6 × 7 =   **h.** 32 ÷ 4 =

   i. 3 × 9 =   **i.** 28 ÷ 7 =

   j. 8 × 4 =   **j.** 54 ÷ 6 =

Product	Pairs of factors	Number of different factors
16	1,16 2,8 4,4	5
9	1,9 3,3	3
12	1,12 2,6 3,4	6
18		

Can you complete the chart Miss West's class has started?

1. Copy and complete this chart.

Product	Pairs of factors	Number of different factors
7		
15		
6		
24		
14		
17		

Miss West told her class that they had been **factoring** numbers. The word *factor* can be used as a noun or a verb.

Noun: A number that is multiplied to give a product. What *factor* is missing in the equation 3 × ___ = 12?

Verb: To find the numbers that have been multiplied to give a product. When you *factor* 9, the result is 1,9 and 3,3.

2. Factor these numbers. Find as many pairs of factors as you can.

    a. 21   **b.** 30   **c.** 40   **d.** 36   **e.** 25   **f.** 48

Pam

Products of 2: 0 , 2 , 4 , 6 , 8 , 10 , 12 , 14 , 16 , 18 , 20
Products of 3: 0 , 3 , 6 , 9 , 12 , 15 , 18 , 21 , 24 , 27 , 30
Products of 4: 0 , 4 , 8 , 12 , 16 , 20 , 24 , 28 , 32 , 36 , 40

There is a special name for the numbers Pam has written.
They are called the **multiples** of 2, the _multiples_ of 3, and
the _multiples_ of 4. The number 10 is a multiple of 2
because 10 is the answer when some number is
multiplied times 2. (The words _multiple_ and _multiply_ go
together.)

1. Write the first 12 multiples of 5.
2. Write the first 12 multiples of 6.
3. Write the first 12 multiples of 7.
4. Write the first 12 multiples of 8.
5. Write the first 12 multiples of 9.
6. Write the first 12 multiples of 10.

7. Write yes or no for each question.

    a. Is 24 a multiple of 8?
    b. Is 40 a multiple of 3?
    c. Is 35 a multiple of 5?
    d. Is 22 a multiple of 7?
    e. Is 14 a multiple of 4?
    f. Is 36 a multiple of 8?
    g. Is 54 a multiple of 6?
    h. Is 120 a multiple of 10?
    i. Is 0 a multiple of every number?

Common multiples

Write the first 12 multiples of 2, 3, 4, 5, and 6 in columns next to each other on your paper.

1. Look at the multiples of 2.
   a. Are all the multiples of 2 even numbers?
   b. Can you see a pattern of the digits in the ones' place? If so, what is it?

2. Look at the multiples of 3.
   a. Are all the multiples of 3 odd numbers?
   b. Can you see a pattern of the digits in the ones' place? If so, what is it?

3. Look at the multiples of 4.
   a. Are all the multiples of 4 even numbers?
   b. Can you see a pattern of the digits in the ones' place? If so, what is it?

4. Look at the multiples of 5.
   a. Are all the multiples of 5 odd numbers?
   b. Can you see a pattern of the digits in the ones' place? If so, what is it?

5. Look at the multiples of 6.
   a. Are all the multiples of 6 even numbers?
   b. Can you see a pattern of the digits in the ones' place? If so, what is it?

6. Mark these numbers in your lists as directed. Answer each question.
   a. Circle all the 12s in red.
   b. Circle all the 15s in blue.
   c. Circle all the 18s in green.
   d. 12 is a multiple of what numbers?
   e. 15 is a multiple of what numbers?
   f. 18 is a multiple of what numbers?

7. 12 is a **common multiple** of 2, 3, 4, and 6 because it is a multiple of each of those numbers.
   a. Find a common multiple of 3, 5, and 6.
   b. Find a common multiple of 2, 4, and 5.
   c. Find a common multiple of 2 and 5.

Even and odd numbers

A class was experimenting with even and odd numbers. Their predictions are written on the chalkboard. They decided that each student should try five examples of each kind to try to prove that their predictions were correct.

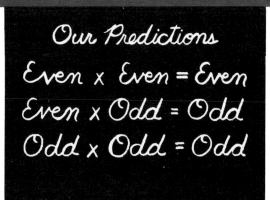

Our Predictions
Even x Even = Even
Even x Odd = Odd
Odd x Odd = Odd

1. Do you think that their predictions are correct?

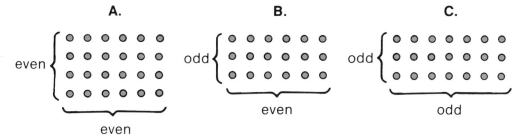

A.

even { (array of dots) } even

B.

odd { (array of dots) } even

C.

odd { (array of dots) } odd

2. Copy these arrays of dots on your paper. Mark as many sets of 2 in each array as you can.

  a. Can all the dots in A be used to make sets of 2? Is there an even number of dots in A?

  b. Can all the dots in B be used to make sets of 2? Is there an even number of dots in B?

  c. Can all the dots in C be used to make sets of 2? Is there an even number of dots in C?

3. Explain why the following statements are true.

  a. An even number multiplied times an even number equals an even number.

  b. An even number multiplied times an odd number equals an even number.

  c. An odd number multiplied times an odd number equals an odd number.

173

There are interesting patterns to be found in our numbers. Try this.

```
0
1
2
3
4
5
6   3
7   2
8   1
9   0
```

1. Write the numbers from 0 through 9 in a column on your paper as shown.
2. Write the same numbers again but put the 0 to the right of the 9 and make your column go from the bottom to the top.
3. Look at the two-digit numbers that you have written. They are multiples of what number?
4. Add the two digits that make up each number. What is the sum of those digits?
5. Multiply 12 times 9. Add the digits that make up the product. What is the sum?

$$23 \times 9 = 207 \qquad 38 \times 9 = 342 \qquad 56 \times 9 = 504$$

6. Add the digits in each of the multiples shown above. What is the sum?

$$83 \times 9 = 747$$

7. Add the digits in the multiple shown above. What is the sum? Add the digits that make up the sum. What is that sum?
8. What do you think is true of the multiples of 9 (except 0×9)?
9. Which of these numbers are the multiples of 9? What is a quick way to find out?

$$351 \qquad 643 \qquad 189 \qquad 423 \qquad 648 \qquad 1206$$

Sometimes you may wish to find the product of three or more factors.

There are four holes in each button. How many holes are there altogether?

2 rows   3 buttons in a row   4 holes in each button

$(2 \times 3) \times 4 =$ $2 \times (3 \times 4) =$
$6 \times 4 = 24$ $2 \times 12 = 24$

There are 24 holes in the buttons.   There are 24 holes in the buttons.

Both students multiplied correctly. It does not matter how you group the factors.

> **Grouping Principle**
> You may group factors in different ways without changing the product.

Find the products. Do each one two ways. Use parentheses to show how you grouped the factors.

1. $3 \times 3 \times 5 =$
2. $4 \times 6 \times 5 =$
3. $6 \times 2 \times 4 =$
4. $8 \times 2 \times 4 =$
5. $3 \times 5 \times 6 =$
6. $4 \times 4 \times 3 =$
7. $8 \times 5 \times 2 =$
8. $6 \times 4 \times 3 =$
9. $7 \times 2 \times 2 =$
10. $5 \times 5 \times 2 =$

Multiplying three factors

Find the total number of items.

Item	Number in a package	Number of packages in a carton	Number of cartons	Total number of items
Gum	5	10	3	
Lifesavers	8	8	4	
Pencils	4	8	6	
Crayons	6	8	2	
Books	5	12	2	
Cups	4	6	5	
Granola bars	2	6	10	
Water glasses	6	4	3	

Something for Fun

Use this chart to help you make up a rule to find the sum of the consecutive odd numbers.

Numbers to be added	Number of numbers to be added	Sum
1	1	1
1 + 3	2	4
1 + 3 + 5	3	9

What is your rule?
    Give the sum of the first 7 odd numbers.
    Give the sum of the first 10 odd numbers.
    Give the sum of the first 12 odd numbers.

1. Give the products.

1 × 2 =	1 × 12 =	1 × 125 =
10 × 2 =	10 × 12 =	10 × 125 =
100 × 2 =	100 × 12 =	100 × 125 =
1,000 × 2 =	1,000 × 12 =	1,000 × 125 =

When we multiply by 10, the digit in the ones' place is always 0. When we multiply by 100, the digits in the ones' and tens' places are always 0. When we multiply by 1,000, what places will always have a 0 in them?

There is a short way to multiply by 10, 100, and 1,000.

$$10 × 5 = 50 \qquad 10 × 75 = 750 \qquad 10 × 842 = 8,420$$

> To multiply by 10: Write the number; then annex one zero.
> (Annex means "place next to.")

$$100 × 5 = 500 \qquad 100 × 75 = 7,500 \qquad 100 × 842 = 84,200$$

> To multiply by 100: Write the number; then annex two zeroes.

$$1,000 × 5 = 5,000 \qquad 1,000 × 75 = 75,000 \qquad 1,000 × 842 = 842,000$$

> To multiply by 1,000: Write the number; then annex three zeroes.

2. Multiply each of these numbers by 10:
36   48   52   567   290

3. Multiply each of these numbers by 100:
62   867   4   90   1,000

4. Multiply each of these numbers by 1,000:
5   71   578   32   10

Multiplying by even tens

The church auditorium has thirty rows of seats with twelve seats in each row. How many seats are there altogether?

$$30 \times 12 = \_\_\_\_$$

You can think of it this way:

$(10 \times 3) \times 12 =$

$10 \times (3 \times 12) =$ $3 \times 12 = 36$ $10 \times 36 = 360$

There are 360 seats.

Give the products.

$40 \times 22 =$	$60 \times 11 =$	$80 \times 12 =$
$(10 \times 4) \times 22 =$	$(10 \times 6) \times 11 =$	$(10 \times 8) \times 12 =$
$10 \times (4 \times 22) =$	$10 \times (6 \times 11) =$	$10 \times (8 \times 12) =$

Look at your products.
What digit is in the ones' place? Will there always be a 0 in the ones' place when you multiply by an even ten (10, 20, 30, 40, . . .)?

There is a short way to write these problems.

Step 1

$$\begin{array}{r} 22 \\ \times\ 40 \\ \hline 0 \end{array}$$

Write a zero in the ones' place.

Step 2

$$\begin{array}{r} 22 \\ \times\ 40 \\ \hline 880 \end{array}$$

Multiply by the number of tens.

Multiply the short way.

1. $\begin{array}{r}22\\ \times\ 40\end{array}$	**2.** $\begin{array}{r}11\\ \times\ 60\end{array}$	**3.** $\begin{array}{r}12\\ \times\ 80\end{array}$	**4.** $\begin{array}{r}\overset{1}{23}\\ \times\ 40\end{array}$	**5.** $\begin{array}{r}17\\ \times\ 30\end{array}$	**6.** $\begin{array}{r}33\\ \times\ 30\end{array}$

Practice

Multiply.

1. 36 × 20	**2.** 64 × 30	**3.** 58 × 20	**4.** 43 × 80	**5.** 69 × 40

6. 29 × 50	**7.** 48 × 70	**8.** 65 × 80	**9.** 12 × 90	**10.** 84 × 30

Name	Heartbeats per minute	Breaths per minute	Blinks per minute
Bill	80	18	11
Jana	83	21	13
Tom	78	17	12

11. About how many times does Bill breathe in 1 hour (60 minutes)?

12. About how many times does Jana's heart beat in 1 hour?

13. About how many times does Tom blink in 1 hour?

14. About how many times does Tom's heart beat in 1 hour?

15. About how many times does Jana blink in 1 hour?

Find this information about yourself if you can.

Multiplication by a two-digit number

The students set up chairs in the school auditorium. They put up twenty-four rows of chairs with twenty-two chairs in each row. How many chairs were there altogether?

$24 \times 22 = $ _____

You can use the multiplication-addition principle to help you find the answer.

How many chairs in four rows?	How many chairs in twenty rows?	How many chairs in twenty-four rows?
22 × 4 ‾‾‾‾ 88	22 × 20 ‾‾‾‾‾ 440	88 + 440 ‾‾‾‾‾ 528

There is a short way to write this.

```
    22
×   24
‾‾‾‾‾‾
    88   (4 × 22)
  440   (20 × 22)
‾‾‾‾‾‾
  528   (24 × 22)
```

We call 88 and 440 *partial products* because each of them is a *part* of the total product. We add them together to find the total product.

Copy and complete.

1. 32
× 23
‾‾‾‾
_____ (3 × 32)
_____ (20 × 32)
_____ (23 × 32)

2. 36
× 42
‾‾‾‾
_____ (2 × 36)
_____ (40 × 36)
_____ (42 × 36)

3. 45
× 64
‾‾‾‾
_____ (4 × 45)
_____ (60 × 45)
_____ (64 × 45)

4. 59
× 26

5. 37
× 45

6. 92
× 53

7. 85
× 42

8. 67
× 53

Using the multiplication-addition principle

A

$$\begin{array}{r} \overset{3}{38} \\ \times\ 24 \\ \hline 2 \end{array} \qquad \begin{array}{r} \overset{\cancel{3}}{38} \\ \times\ 24 \\ \hline 2 \end{array}$$

Explain what was done in A.
a. Why was the small 3 written?

b. Why was the small 3 crossed off?

c. $4 \times 38 = ?$

B

$$\begin{array}{r} \overset{\cancel{3}}{38} \\ \times\ 24 \\ \hline 152 \\ 0 \end{array} \qquad \begin{array}{r} \overset{1\cancel{3}}{38} \\ \times\ 24 \\ \hline 152 \\ 60 \end{array} \qquad \begin{array}{r} \overset{1\cancel{3}}{38} \\ \times\ 24 \\ \hline 152 \\ 760 \end{array}$$

Explain what was done in B.
a. Why was a zero placed in the ones' place?

b. $20 \times 38 = ?$

C

$$\begin{array}{r} 38 \\ \times\ 24 \\ \hline 152 \\ 760 \\ \hline 912 \end{array}$$

Explain what was done in C.
a. Why were 152 and 760 added?

b. $24 \times 38 = ?$

c. What principle was used to help solve this problem?

Solve.

1. $\begin{array}{r}23\\ \times\ 16\\ \hline\end{array}$	**2.** $\begin{array}{r}46\\ \times\ 45\\ \hline\end{array}$	**3.** $\begin{array}{r}17\\ \times\ 56\\ \hline\end{array}$	**4.** $\begin{array}{r}35\\ \times\ 36\\ \hline\end{array}$	**5.** $\begin{array}{r}95\\ \times\ 23\\ \hline\end{array}$
6. $\begin{array}{r}29\\ \times\ 54\\ \hline\end{array}$	**7.** $\begin{array}{r}82\\ \times\ 63\\ \hline\end{array}$	**8.** $\begin{array}{r}48\\ \times\ 77\\ \hline\end{array}$	**9.** $\begin{array}{r}75\\ \times\ 25\\ \hline\end{array}$	**10.** $\begin{array}{r}83\\ \times\ 19\\ \hline\end{array}$

Two-digit multiplication

Explain how this problem was solved. What numerals are missing?

```
    79
×   47
   5□3
  □□60
 3,713
```

What was added to 49? Why?

What was added to 28? Why?

Some students cannot work this kind of multiplication problem quickly because they have trouble adding the tens they renamed to the new product.

1. Give the answers aloud. Do not write the problems.

   a. Add 6 to each number: 21, 35, 54, 36, 18, 42, 27, 49

   b. Add 8 to each number: 28, 24, 16, 49, 63, 72, 81, 45

   c. Add 7 to each number: 14, 56, 48, 63, 32, 27, 81, 25

   d. Add 9 to each number: 72, 27, 63, 24, 35, 18, 49, 56

   e. Add 5 to each number: 48, 16, 27, 15, 24, 37, 49, 12

   Practice this kind of addition until you can do it very quickly.

2. Solve.

a. 59	**b.** 38	**c.** 85	**d.** 77	**e.** 84
× 78	× 67	× 49	× 86	× 67

f. 69	**g.** 87	**h.** 35	**i.** 76	**j.** 28
× 28	× 46	× 89	× 87	× 49

Practice

What numerals are missing?

```
    264
  ×  58
  21□2
 13□0□
 1□31□
```

Solve.

1. 136
× 32

2. 264
× 50

3. 156
× 47

4. 526
× 42

5. 165
× 38

6. 524
× 72

7. 363
× 24

8. 501
× 63

9. 824
× 56

10. 432
× 67

11. 265
× 19

12. 916
× 45

13. 286
× 70

14. 732
× 48

15. 265
× 37

16. 300
× 24

17. 260
× 15

18. 743
× 90

19. 306
× 82

20. 157
× 27

183

A. Forty-four boys want to play soccer. Eleven players make one team. How many teams can be made?

$44 \div 11 = 4$

There can be four teams.

B. Thirty-six girls want to play kickball. They formed four teams. How many girls were on each team?

$36 \div 4 = 9$

There were nine girls on each team.

How are these division problems different?

a. What does the dividend in A tell us? in B?

b. What does the divisor in A tell us? in B?

c. What does the quotient in A tell us? in B?

Give the quotients.

1. $24 \div 8 =$	**9.** $54 \div 6 =$	**17.** $15 \div 3 =$
2. $45 \div 5 =$	**10.** $48 \div 8 =$	**18.** $14 \div 2 =$
3. $63 \div 7 =$	**11.** $12 \div 6 =$	**19.** $21 \div 3 =$
4. $42 \div 6 =$	**12.** $18 \div 9 =$	**20.** $30 \div 6 =$
5. $35 \div 7 =$	**13.** $24 \div 4 =$	**21.** $49 \div 7 =$
6. $28 \div 4 =$	**14.** $36 \div 9 =$	**22.** $72 \div 9 =$
7. $18 \div 6 =$	**15.** $40 \div 8 =$	**23.** $64 \div 8 =$
8. $32 \div 8 =$	**16.** $50 \div 5 =$	**24.** $36 \div 4 =$

Write a story problem for each of these equations.

a. $45 \div 5 =$ _____ Make this one like problem A above.

b. $24 \div 6 =$ _____ Make this one like problem B above.

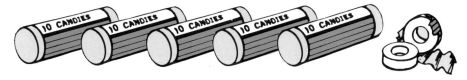

Jerry had 52 candies. He wanted to divide them evenly between two of his friends. How many candies would each friend receive?

$$52 \div 2 = \underline{\hphantom{00}}$$

Andy   Bill

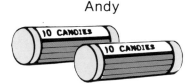 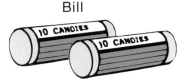

$$\begin{array}{r} 2 \\ 2{\overline{\smash{)}52}} \\ -4 \\ \hline 1 \end{array}$$

First, Jerry gave each friend two packages of ten candies.

a. How many packages of ten candies did he give away?

b. How many packages of ten candies did he have left?

$$\begin{array}{r} 2 \\ 2{\overline{\smash{)}52}} \\ -4 \\ \hline 12 \end{array}$$

Next, Jerry opened the other package of ten candies. He put the other two candies with those ten.

c. How many candies does Jerry have now?

Andy   Bill

$$\begin{array}{r} 26 \\ 2{\overline{\smash{)}52}} \\ -4 \\ \hline 12 \\ -12 \\ \hline 0 \end{array}$$

Then Jerry gave each of his friends six candies.

d. How many candies did he give away this time?

e. How many candies does he have left?

f. How many candies did each friend receive?

$$72 \div 3 = \underline{\quad}$$

Step 1 Divide the tens.	Step 2 Multiply and subtract.	Step 3 Rename the remaining tens as ones. Add the ones.	Step 4 Divide the ones. Multiply and subtract.

```
      2              2              2             24
   3)72           3)72           3)72          3)72
                   -6             -6            -6
                    1             12            12
                                               -12
                                                 0
```

Explain each step.

```
      1              1              1             16
   4)64           4)64           4)64          4)64
                   -4             -4            -4
                    2             24            24
                                               -24
                                                 0
```

Solve.

1. 3)42
2. 7)91
3. 6)84
4. 5)65
5. 2)38

6. 7)98
7. 6)96
8. 4)72
9. 5)85
10. 3)51

11. 6)78
12. 2)32
13. 3)48
14. 5)95
15. 4)76

Division with remainders

Mrs. Kane had seventy-seven cookies to give to her three neighbors. If she gave the same number of cookies to each neighbor, how many would each get? How many would Mrs. Kane have left?

$$77 \div 3 = \underline{}$$

Step 1	**Step 2**	**Step 3**
Divide the tens. Multiply and subtract.	Rename the remaining tens as ones. Add the other ones.	Divide the ones. Multiply and subtract.

$$
\begin{array}{r} 2 \\ 3\overline{)77} \\ -6 \\ \hline 1 \end{array}
\qquad
\begin{array}{r} 2 \\ 3\overline{)77} \\ -6 \\ \hline 17 \end{array}
\qquad
\begin{array}{r} 25 \\ 3\overline{)77} \\ -6 \\ \hline 17 \\ -15 \\ \hline 2r \end{array}
$$

Each neighbor would receive twenty-five cookies. Mrs. Kane would have two left.

Examine these examples. What numerals are missing?

$$
\begin{array}{r} 49 \\ 2\overline{)98} \\ -\square \\ \hline 18 \\ -1\square \\ \hline 0 \end{array}
\qquad
\begin{array}{r} 2\square \\ 4\overline{)95} \\ -8 \\ \hline 15 \\ -\square\square \\ \hline \square r \end{array}
\qquad
\begin{array}{r} \square 2 \\ 4\overline{)89} \\ -8 \\ \hline 09 \\ -\ \square \\ \hline 1r \end{array}
\qquad
\begin{array}{r} \square 0 \\ 3\overline{)90} \\ -\square \\ \hline 00 \\ -\ 0 \\ \hline 0 \end{array}
$$

Solve.

1. $2\overline{)73}$ 2. $5\overline{)92}$ 3. $3\overline{)99}$ 4. $4\overline{)95}$ 5. $4\overline{)72}$

6. $3\overline{)81}$ 7. $2\overline{)77}$ 8. $2\overline{)87}$ 9. $4\overline{)80}$ 10. $3\overline{)69}$

11. $5\overline{)88}$ 12. $3\overline{)68}$ 13. $2\overline{)70}$ 14. $6\overline{)82}$ 15. $4\overline{)87}$

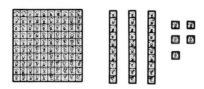

Janice had 135 stamps to put on 3 pages of her stamp book. If she put the same number of stamps on each, how many stamps would Janice put on each page?

135 ÷ 3 = _____

```
    4
3)135
 -12
   1
```

Janice tore her sheet of 100 stamps into strips of ten stamps.

a. How many strips of 10 stamps did she have then?

b. How many strips of 10 stamps could she put on each page?

c. How many strips of 10 stamps would be left?

```
    45
3)135
 -12
   15
 - 15
```

Janice tore the strip of 10 stamps apart and put the other 5 stamps with them.

d. How many single stamps did she have then?

e. How many single stamps could she put on each page?

f. Are there any single stamps left?

g. How many stamps altogether are on each page?

Solve.

1. 4)232   **2.** 6)156   **3.** 3)165   **4.** 5)105   **5.** 3)117

188

Estimating quotients

There is room for eight persons to sit at each table in the cafeteria. About how many tables will be needed to seat 300 persons? Look at the chart to help you estimate the answer.

Will 10 tables be needed? 20? 30? 40? Between 30 and 40 tables will be needed.

10 × 8 = 80	60 × 8 = 480
20 × 8 = 160	70 × 8 = 560
30 × 8 = 240	80 × 8 = 640
40 × 8 = 320	90 × 8 = 720
50 × 8 = 400	100 × 8 = 800

1. Estimate the quotients.

a. $8\overline{)534}$　　b. $8\overline{)426}$　　c. $8\overline{)100}$　　d. $8\overline{)623}$

2. Make a multiplication chart to help you estimate these quotients.

a. $4\overline{)153}$　　b. $4\overline{)234}$　　c. $4\overline{)315}$　　d. $4\overline{)98}$

3. Make a multiplication chart to help you estimate these quotients.

a. $6\overline{)434}$　　b. $6\overline{)345}$　　c. $6\overline{)193}$　　d. $6\overline{)278}$

4. Estimate these quotients. Do not make a multiplication chart.

Example: $5\overline{)340}$　　60 × 5 = 300　　Between 60 and 70.
　　　　　　　　　　　　70 × 5 = 350

a. $3\overline{)205}$　　b. $7\overline{)152}$　　c. $9\overline{)754}$　　d. $5\overline{)328}$

189

Divide.

1.
2)174

2.
3)195

3.
4)236

4.
6)354

5.
7)182

6.
5)345

7.
8)432

8.
5)305

9.
6)360

10.
4)272

11.
6)294

12.
4)204

13.
7)574

14.
2)186

15.
7)350

Faith Christian School planned a Cookie Day for a children's home nearby. The cookies were put in small plastic bags so that they would be easy to serve to the children. The fourth grade class was in charge of bagging the cookies. They made a chart to show what they did.
Complete the chart.

Kind of cookie	Number of cookies	Number put in each bag	Number of bags needed	Number of cookies left
Chocolate chip	138	4		
Peanut butter	75	3		
Snickerdoodles	92	3		
Krispie treats	125	2		
Gingersnaps	143	3		
Honey drops	65	2		

a. How many bags were prepared altogether?
b. How many cookies were left over? (The fourth-grade students ate the leftovers.)
c. There were how many more bags of Krispie treats than bags of gingersnaps?

Checking division

It is important to check your answers to make sure that
they are right.

Examine these problems to see if they have been solved
correctly.

A. $\dfrac{9}{8)72}$ **B.** $\dfrac{7}{7)42}$ **C.** $\dfrac{7}{8)56}$ **D.** $\dfrac{6}{3)24}$

How did you know that problems A and C are correct?
How did you know that problems B and D are incorrect?
Did you multiply the divisor and the quotient and then
check to see if that answer equaled the dividend?

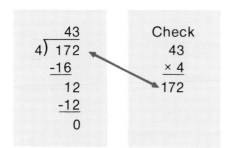

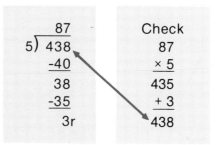

```
    43              Check
4) 172              43
  -16              × 4
   12              172
  -12
    0
```

```
    87              Check
5) 438              87
  -40              × 5
   38              435
  -35              + 3
   3r              438
```

You can check a division problem by multiplying the
divisor and the quotient. That answer should equal the
dividend. If there is a remainder, add it to the product
before you compare with the dividend.

Check each of these problems. Tell which are correct.

1.
```
    57
7)394
 -35
   44
 -42
   2r
```
2.
```
    87
8)698
 -64
   58
 -56
   2r
```
3.
```
    81
5)355
 -35
   05
  - 5
    0
```
4.
```
    63
6)376
 -36
   16
 -16
    0
```
5.
```
    44
7)324
 -28
   34
 -28
   6r
```

Solve and check.

6. $8)\overline{647}$ **7.** $5)\overline{467}$ **8.** $3)\overline{294}$ **9.** $6)\overline{327}$ **10.** $2)\overline{185}$

Solve and check.

1.
3)285

2.
4)95

3.
6)450

4.
3)258

5.
7)438

6.
9)147

7.
8)253

8.
4)167

9.
6)350

10.
9)369

11.
2)176

12.
5)323

13.
6)431

14.
7)293

15.
5)154

16.
8)360

17.
4)381

18.
3)175

19.
7)421

20.
6)402

Copy the problem. Solve.
Fill in the missing digit so that the remainder will be 0.

21.
4)35□

22.
6)23□

23.
5)34□

24.
7)43□

25.
8)13□

Something for Fun

Mr. Kross makes three-legged stools and four-legged tables. One day he noticed that what he had completed that day had 31 legs. How many stools and how many tables did he make that day? (There are three possible answers.)

More division

This carton holds 8 light bulbs. How many cartons would be needed to package 3,376 light bulbs?

$$3,376 \div 8 = \underline{}$$

Step 1	**Step 2**	**Step 3**
Divide the hundreds.	Divide the tens.	Divide the ones.
Multiply and subtract.	Multiply and subtract.	Multiply and subtract.

```
      4                42                 422
 8)3,376           8)3,376            8)3,376
  -32               - 32               - 32
    1                 17                 17
                    -16                -16
                      1                  16
                                       -16
                                         0
```

It would take 422 cartons.

Explain how these examples were solved. What numerals are missing?

```
    1□9                □1□                8□2
 4)516              6)1,272           9)7,490
  -4                 -1 2              -□□
   11                 0 7               29
   -8                 -6               -27
    3□                 □□               20
   -36                -12              -18
     □                  □               □r
```

Divide.

1. 5)1,630

2. 7)1,834

3. 6)3,925

4. 4)1,152

5. 9)1,999

6. 8)923

7. 7)3,661

8. 2)928

9. 3)583

10. 6)1,452

11. 4)582

12. 6)748

Practice

This chart shows what was done in a fruit packing shed in one day. Complete the chart.

Kind of fruit	Number of pounds	Number of pounds per bag	Number of bags
Red Delicious	2,912	8	
Yellow Delicious	2,160	5	
Winesap	1,500	5	
Rome Beauty		8	255
Jonathan	1,488	6	

Divide and check.

1. 7)3,492

2. 5)630

3. 4)848

4. 9)1,629

5. 3)1,464

6. 6)789

7. 2)1,538

8. 8)968

9. 5)3,495

10. 6)1,386

11. 5)4,620

12. 3)1,186

Sensible quotients

Heritage Christian Elementary School pledged to raise $648 to send to a Christian school in Mexico. Mrs. Brown's class was trying to find out how much each of the six grades must collect. Some students thought the answer was $18. Others said the answer was $108. They said that $18 was not a sensible answer.

Which answer do you think is right?

$$
\begin{array}{r}
18 \\
6\overline{)648} \\
-6 \\
\hline 048 \\
48 \\
\hline
\end{array}
$$

$$
\begin{array}{r}
108 \\
6\overline{)648} \\
-6 \\
\hline 048 \\
-48 \\
\hline
\end{array}
$$

Estimate. Tell if the quotients given are sensible.

Example:

$$
\begin{array}{r}
45 \\
3\overline{)1,215}
\end{array}
$$

Between 400 and 500—45 is not sensible.

1.
$$
\begin{array}{r}
508 \\
6\overline{)3,048}
\end{array}
$$

2.
$$
\begin{array}{r}
330 \\
7\overline{)2,310}
\end{array}
$$

3.
$$
\begin{array}{r}
42 \\
9\overline{)3,618}
\end{array}
$$

4.
$$
\begin{array}{r}
213 \\
8\overline{)1,704}
\end{array}
$$

5.
$$
\begin{array}{r}
18 \\
4\overline{)432}
\end{array}
$$

6.
$$
\begin{array}{r}
79 \\
8\overline{)632}
\end{array}
$$

7.
$$
\begin{array}{r}
521 \\
5\overline{)2,605}
\end{array}
$$

8.
$$
\begin{array}{r}
92 \\
7\overline{)644}
\end{array}
$$

9.
$$
\begin{array}{r}
409 \\
3\overline{)1,227}
\end{array}
$$

10.
$$
\begin{array}{r}
82 \\
9\overline{)738}
\end{array}
$$

11.
$$
\begin{array}{r}
16 \\
6\overline{)636}
\end{array}
$$

12.
$$
\begin{array}{r}
604 \\
2\overline{)1,208}
\end{array}
$$

Quotients with zeroes

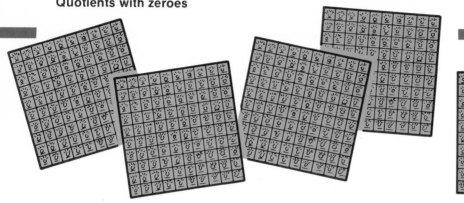

412 ÷ 4 = _____

Imagine that you have 412 stamps to divide into four groups.

a. How many sheets of 100 could you put into each group?

b. Would there be any sheets of 100 left?

c. How many strips of 10 could you put into each group?

```
      10
  4)412
    -4
     01
```

Now imagine that you tear the strip of 10 apart and put the single stamps with them.

d. How many single stamps would you have?

e. How many single stamps could you put into each group?

```
     103
  4)412
    -4
     012
    - 12
       0
```

Explain how these problems were solved. What numerals are missing?

```
    107            □02             601
 6)642          8)3,216         3)1,803
  -6             -3 2             -□□
   042             016             003
  - □□            - 16            - 3
     0               0               0
```

Solve.

1.
$$7)\overline{3,514}$$

2.
$$6)\overline{4,224}$$

3.
$$8)\overline{4,832}$$

4.
$$4)\overline{2,804}$$

1. Solve and check.

a. 3,216 ÷ 8 =

b. 2,406 ÷ 6 =

c. 1,324 ÷ 2 =

d. 5,963 ÷ 7 =

e. 1,634 ÷ 4 =

f. 3,155 ÷ 5 =

g. 8,316 ÷ 9 =

h. 4,545 ÷ 5 =

i. 5,231 ÷ 6 =

j. 3,622 ÷ 4 =

k. 7,218 ÷ 9 =

l. 6,408 ÷ 8 =

m. 1,324 ÷ 5 =

n. 829 ÷ 2 =

o. 3,333 ÷ 6 =

p. 7,260 ÷ 8 =

q. 1,342 ÷ 6 =

r. 2,514 ÷ 4 =

s. 1,726 ÷ 5 =

t. 4,332 ÷ 6 =

2. Find the length of one side of each polygon. Estimate your answer before you begin.

a.

Perimeter: 816 m

b.

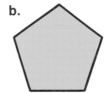

Perimeter: 2,935 ft.

c.

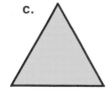

Perimeter: 924 cm

d.

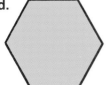

Perimeter: 2,412 in.

e.

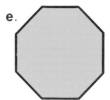

Perimeter: 3,240 yd.

1. Factor these numbers. Give as many pairs of factors as possible.
   a. 32   **b.** 12   **c.** 36   **d.** 30   **e.** 24

2. Choose the correct numbers.
   a. Multiples of 8: 8   34   40   63   72
   b. Multiples of 4: 0   18   24   36   42
   c. Multiples of 7: 22   17   47   63   84

3. Which is an example of the grouping principle for multiplication?
   a. $3 \times 5 = 5 \times 3$ **b.** $(3 \times 4) \times 8 = 3 \times (4 \times 8)$
   c. $3 \times (10 + 2) = (3 \times 10) + (3 \times 2)$

4. What is the short way to multiply a number by ten?

5. How many marbles are in 15 bags when each bag holds 36 marbles?

   Meg did it this way:

36	36	360	540 marbles
$\times\ 10$	$\times\ 5$	$+\ 180$	
360	180	540	

   What math principle did she use?

6. Solve.

   a. 36   **b.** 45   **c.** 26   **d.** 38   **e.** 246
   $\times\ 20$ $\times\ 80$ $\times\ 24$ $\times\ 19$ $\times\ 15$

7. Solve. (There may be a remainder.)
   a. $36 \div 2 =$ **b.** $145 \div 5 =$ **c.** $525 \div 5 =$ **d.** $3{,}426 \div 8 =$

8. Mrs. Crane has a package of 255 sheets of paper. If her three children share the paper equally, how many sheets will each child get?

9. Mrs. Bell gave each of her three children 49 sheets of paper. How many sheets of paper did she give them altogether?

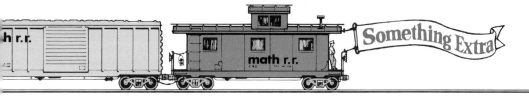

Lattice Multiplication

There are several ways to solve multiplication problems. Here is one used hundreds of years ago. We think it is the way Christopher Columbus multiplied, because it was found in a book that was used in Italy about the time he lived.

This kind of multiplication is often called lattice multiplication because the frame looks something like a lattice when it is finished.

$$43 \times 68 = \underline{\hphantom{000}}$$

1. Write the factors outside the frame as shown.

2. Multiply 4 × 8. Write the tens' digit of the product in the top part of the space and the ones' digit in the bottom part of the space.

3. Continue multiplying the pairs of factors: 4 × 6, 3 × 8, 3 × 6. Write the products in the proper spaces as in step 2.

4. Add the digits in the slanted columns, starting at the bottom right-hand corner. Carry as necessary.

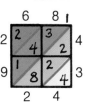

5. The answer is read down and to the right.

   43 × 68 = 2,924

   2,924

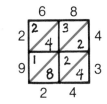

Try these:
   a. 38 × 77 =   **b.** 86 × 64 =   **c.** 93 × 45 =

199

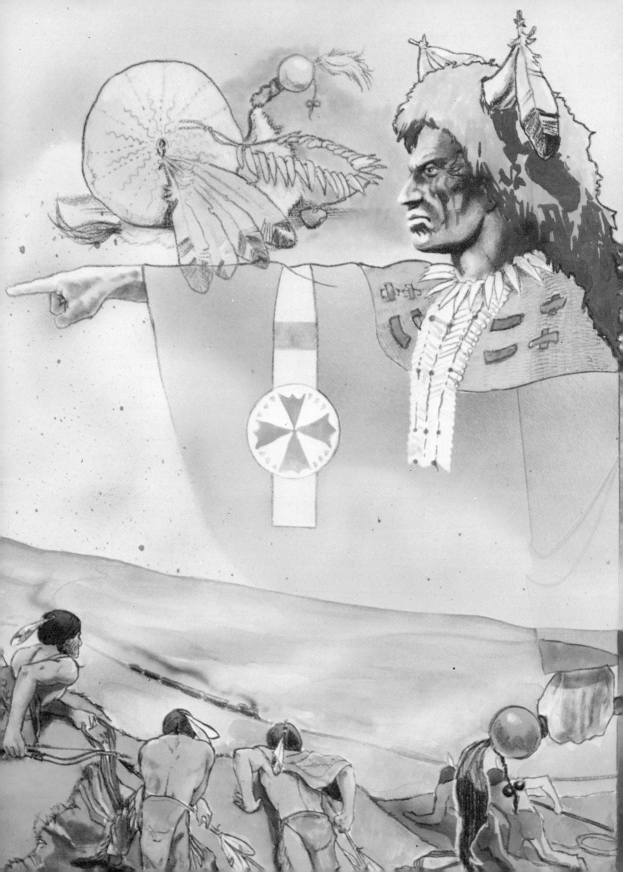

Unit 7

Capturing the Iron Horse

Not everyone approved of the coming of the railroad. The Indians of the Great Plains hated the railroad's smoke and noise, and even more, they hated the white men who killed the buffalo and built towns and farms on Indian land. Since the trains brought the white men, some Indians began to believe that stopping the trains would mean saving the land they loved.

By the 1860s, the hatred of white men and their railroad had become a central part of the Indian religion. Indians would pray and make sacrifices and vows to their gods to drive out the white men. Some would even fast and pray to their gods until they fell into a trance, during which they would dream about how to destroy the white invaders.

One medicine man fell into such a trance and saw a vision of how to destroy the railroads. In this vision, he was told to make a strong rawhide rope and bless it through a special ceremony. Then he was to command warriors on horses to hold the rope across the track. On the appointed day, he ordered the warriors of his tribe to tie the rope to their horses and to brace themselves on either side of the track as if ready for a tug-of-war. The medicine man was sure that the train would be stopped by the "magic rope" and the land would be returned to the Indians. His faith was strong, but it was misplaced. As the great engine sped across the plain toward the rope, the warriors drew the rope even tighter, confident that they would achieve great glory. They lost their assurance only when the engine reached the rope and began to drag them along the plain and toward the great wheels.

Many warriors and horses were killed by the great locomotive that day. They had trusted in the wrong thing. The Indians' failure was not because of a lack of education, intelligence, or sincerity. Their failure was the result of the same mistake that many lost people make today. They believe in something that has no power to save. (See I Timothy 2:5.)

201

Goals for Unit 7

1. I will learn more special words for geometry.
2. I will learn to find the area of a region.
3. I will learn to find the volume of a solid figure.
4. I will learn more about symmetry.

Words to Remember

geometry	area
ray	square unit
angle	similar
right angle	congruent
point of intersection	solid figure
perpendicular	volume
parallel	cubic unit
parallelogram	symmetry

What do you remember?

1. Name the line segments that form the sides of these figures.

   a.

   b.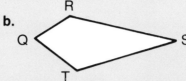

2. Which of these angles are right angles?

   a. 　　**b.** 　　**c.**

3. Find the area of these regions.

   a. 　　**b.** 　　**c.**

4. Which figure is similar to the first one in the row?

5. Which figure is congruent to the first one in the row?

6. Find the volume.

We see many beautiful designs in the world that God has created.

We see designs and patterns in the things men build.

The word **geometry** means "earth measurement." Geometry was once used to find the boundaries and sizes of land. Today it helps us study and understand many other things about our world. Part of geometry is the study of points, lines, and the figures they form.

204

Rays

We use many special words when we study geometry.
You know some of them already.

point   ●
line   ←——————→ Goes on and on in both directions
line segment ●————————● Shortest path between two points
region   Space inside a closed figure

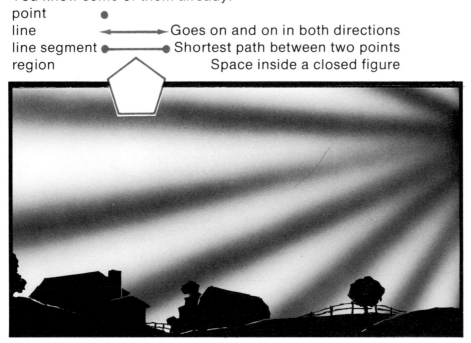

The streams of light coming from the sun are sometimes
called *rays* of sunlight. This can help us remember the
meaning of another special word in geometry—**ray**. A ray
is a part of a line. It has one endpoint but it goes on and
on in one direction.

A   B $\overrightarrow{A\ B}$ Ray AB
●—————————●———→

Remember to say the endpoint first when naming a ray.
Name these rays.

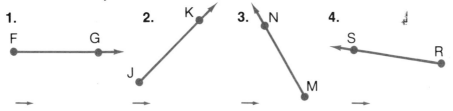

1.

F   G
●—————————●——→

→

2. K

J

→

3. N

M

→

4. S   R

←

→

Angle A

When two rays have the same endpoint, they form an **angle**. The angle shown above is called Angle A (or Angle BAC or Angle CAB).

1. Name the rays that form this angle.

2. One angle in this drawing is ∠RTS. Name three other angles.

Look around the room you are in to find examples of angles. Examine the corners of this clock. They are a special kind of angle called a **right angle**. They are like the corners of a square.

3. Which of these are right angles?

4. How many right angles are there in each of these drawings?

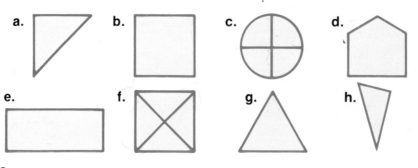

Intersecting lines

You know that the place where two streets cross is called an intersection. That word is used in geometry too. The point where lines cross is called the **point of intersection**.

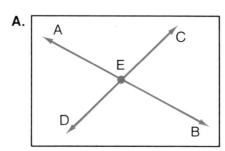

$\overleftrightarrow{AB}$ and $\overleftrightarrow{CD}$ *intersect* at point E.

If the angles formed by two intersecting lines are right angles, the lines are **perpendicular**. In Picture B, $\overleftrightarrow{FG}$ is perpendicular to $\overrightarrow{HI}$.

1. Name the angles in Picture A.
2. Name the angles in Picture B.
3. Which of these lines are perpendicular to each other?

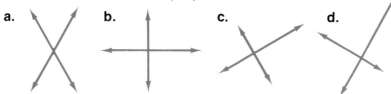

a.   **b.**   **c.**   **d.**

The Bible talks about a plumbline in Amos 7:7: "Thus he shewed me: and, behold, the Lord stood upon a wall made by a plumbline, with a plumbline in His hand."
A plumbline makes sure the wall is perpendicular to the ground. The Bible is God's plumbline to help us see if we are *upright* in our hearts. (Isaiah 28:17)

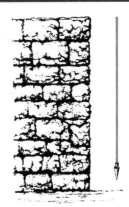

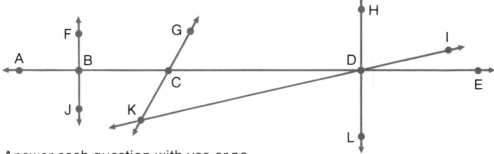

Answer each question with yes or no.

1. Is ∠ABF a right angle?
2. Is $\overleftrightarrow{HL}$ perpendicular to $\overleftrightarrow{AE}$?
3. Do $\overleftrightarrow{FJ}$ and $\overleftrightarrow{HL}$ intersect?
4. Is ∠CKD a right angle?
5. Do $\overleftrightarrow{KI}$ and $\overleftrightarrow{AE}$ intersect?
6. Is $\overleftrightarrow{GK}$ perpendicular to $\overleftrightarrow{KI}$?

7. 36	**8.** 872	**9.** 789	**10.** 387	**11.** 923
58	967	199	176	888
+ 27	+ 453	+ 583	+ 246	+ 629

12. 398	**13.** 2,000	**14.** 4,531	**15.** 509	**16.** 901
- 109	- 1,645	- 1,842	- 183	- 763

17. 36	**18.** 851	**19.** 295	**20.** 316	**21.** 500
× 42	× 63	× 57	× 89	× 22

Parallel lines

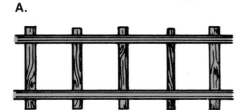
A.

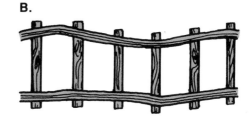
B.

It is important that the rails of a railroad track be the same distance apart for their entire length. Can you imagine what would happen if rails were like those in picture B?

The rails in picture A are an example of **parallel lines.** Parallel lines are two lines that are always the same distance apart. They do not intersect.

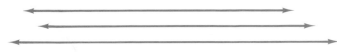

Line segments may also be parallel.

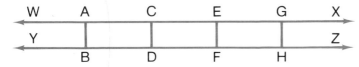

Complete each statement with **a.** is perpendicular to
b. intersects, or
c. is parallel to.

1. $\overleftrightarrow{AB}$ _____ $\overleftrightarrow{CD}$
2. $\overleftrightarrow{XZ}$ _____ $\overleftrightarrow{CD}$
3. $\overleftrightarrow{AC}$ _____ $\overleftrightarrow{CD}$
4. $\overleftrightarrow{WY}$ _____ $\overleftrightarrow{AB}$
5. $\overline{MN}$ _____ $\overline{KL}$
6. $\overleftrightarrow{AB}$ _____ $\overline{BD}$
7. $\overline{IJ}$ _____ $\overline{BD}$
8. $\overleftrightarrow{WY}$ _____ $\overleftrightarrow{XZ}$
9. $\overline{EF}$ _____ $\overline{GH}$
10. $\overline{BD}$ _____ $\overleftrightarrow{CD}$

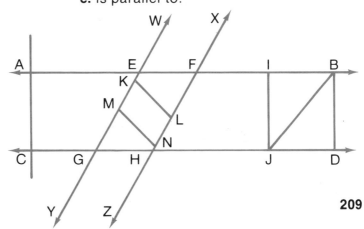

You already know the names of many kinds of polygons.

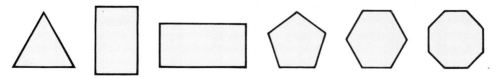

This polygon is called a **parallelogram.** Notice that the opposite sides are parallel.

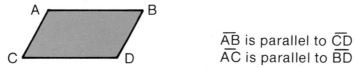

$\overline{AB}$ is parallel to $\overline{CD}$
$\overline{AC}$ is parallel to $\overline{BD}$

1. Which of these polygons are parallelograms?

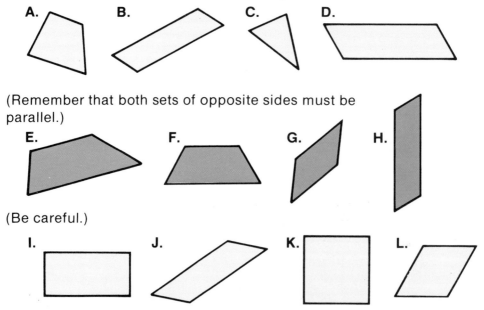

(Remember that both sets of opposite sides must be parallel.)

(Be careful.)

2. Think about these statements. Which ones are true?
  a. The opposite sides of a rectangle are parallel.
  b. A rectangle is a special kind of parallelogram.
  c. A square is a special kind of rectangle.
  d. A parallelogram must have four right angles.

Naming polygons

1. Which of these polygons are parallelograms?
2. Which of these polygons are rectangles?
3. Which of these polygons are squares?
4. Which of these polygons are triangles?

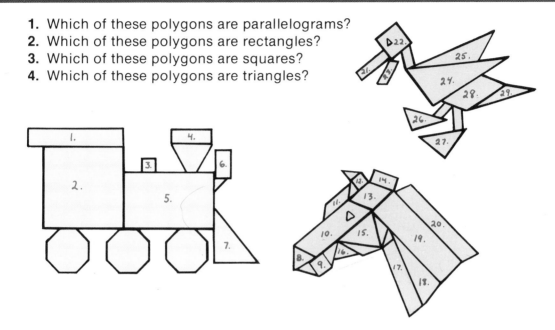

5. Explain why this polygon is a square, a rectangle, and a parallelogram.

6. Select five points on a piece of paper. Make sure they are scattered out like those below. Use a ruler or straightedge to connect every two points. How many segments will you make after all points are connected?

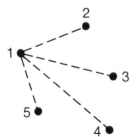

Do you remember?

1. Which is a line segment?

   a.   **b.**   **c.**

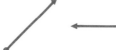

2. Which are rays?

   a.   **b.**   **c.**

3. Which is a right angle?

   a.   **b.**   **c.**

4. Which are intersecting lines?

   a.   **b.**   **c.**

5. Which are parallel lines?

   a.   **b.**   **c.**

6. Which is *not* a polygon?

   a.   **b.**   **c.**

7. Which are perpendicular lines?

   a.   **b.**   **c.**

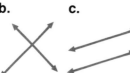

8. Which is *not* a parallelogram?

   a.   **b.**   **c.**

9. Which has a right angle?

   a.   **b.**   **c.**

10. Which are rectangles?

   a.   **b.**   **c.**

Area of a region

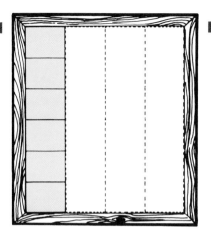

Mrs. White is covering the bulletin board with construction paper squares. She has put six squares along one side of the board. The dotted lines show how many rows of squares she needs to cover the whole board.

a. How many rows of six squares are needed?

b. How many squares are needed altogether?

$4 \times 6 =$ _____ squares

When we measure a region, we say that we are finding the **area** of that region. We use **square units.**

1. Find the area of these regions by counting.

a.
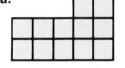

b.

c.

d.
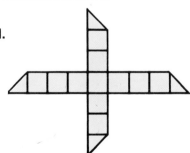

e.
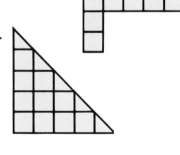

2. Find the area of these regions by multiplying.

a.
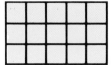

b.

c.

Finding area by multiplying

Mr. Walker is going to plant grass in his backyard. The bag of grass seed says that there is enough to plant an area of 250 square meters. Is one bag of seed enough for his yard?

a. How many square meters will there be in one row along the side of the yard?

b. How many rows will there be?

c. How many square meters are there altogether?

d. Is one bag of seed enough?

Find the area of these regions.

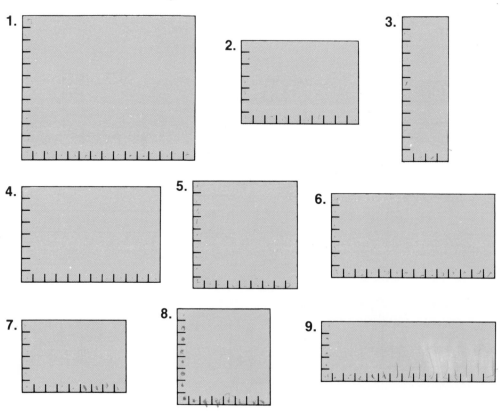

Solving problems

Draw a picture to help you solve each of these problems.
Ask yourself these questions:
> How many square units are in one row?
> How many rows of square units are there?
> How many square units are there altogether?

1. Gina was making a gift for her mother. She glued small tiles on a piece of wood. It was to protect a table from hot dishes. The piece of wood was 10 centimeters wide and 15 centimeters long. Each tile covered 1 square centimeter. How many tiles did Gina need?

2. Jennifer's father asked her to paint the top of the Ping-Pong table. It was 5 feet wide and 9 feet long. The label on the can of paint said there was enough paint to cover an area of 75 square feet. Was one can of paint enough to paint the table?

3. Mr. Turner bought carpet squares for the floor of the hall. Each square covered one square foot. The hall was 5 feet wide and 36 feet long. How many carpet squares did he need?

4. Lane wanted to raise some chickens. He decided to have an area of at least 2 square meters for each bird. He had room to make a chicken yard that was 4 meters wide and 9 meters long. How many chickens could he plan to buy?

5. The Fultons were shopping for carpet for David's room. The room was 3 meters wide and 4 meters long. How many square meters of carpet did they need? The kind of carpet David liked cost $15 a square meter. How much would his carpet cost altogether?

6. Miss Conley's class had a pizza party. The pizzas were made in rectangular pans instead of round ones. The pizzas were cut into different sizes. The cheese pizzas were cut into pieces 4 inches wide and 6 inches long. The pepperoni pizzas were cut into pieces 3 inches wide and 8 inches long. The sausage pizzas were cut into pieces 5 inches wide and 5 inches long. Which pieces were the biggest?

1. Find the area of these regions by counting. Give the answers to the nearest whole square unit.

a. 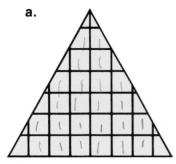 **b.** 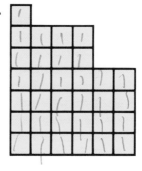 **c.**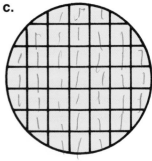

2. Find the area of these regions by multiplying.

a.  **b.**   **c.**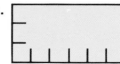

d.   **e.**   **f.**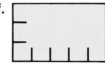

3. Guess which of these regions has the greatest area.
Guess which of these regions has the least area.
Find the areas to see if you are right.

a.  **b.**   **c.**

Can you trust your eyes?

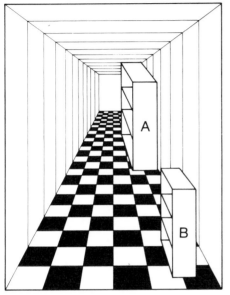

Which of these shelves is larger, shelf A or shelf B?

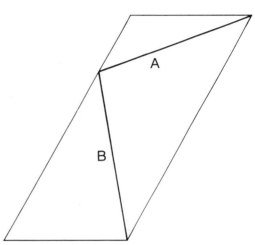

Which is longer, line segment A or line segment B?

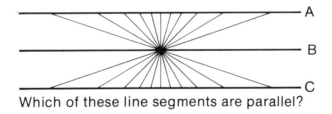

Which of these line segments are parallel?

We cannot always trust our eyes. We can be fooled. But we do not have to be fooled. We can train ourselves to observe carefully and to use measuring tools such as meter sticks and tape measures.

Sometimes in life we can be fooled into thinking something is right when it is really wrong. But we do not have to be fooled in this way either. We have the Bible for our "measuring tool" to tell us what is right or wrong. We must *learn* what it says and then be willing to *do* what it says.

Similar figures

Examine these polygons. Can you see that they all have the same shape? When figures have the same shape, we say that they are **similar**.

Which polygons are similar?

1. **a.** **b.**  **c.** **d.**

2. **a.** **b.** **c.** **d.**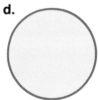

3. **a.** **b.** **c.**  **d.**

4. **a.** **b.** **c.** **d.**

218

Congruent figures

 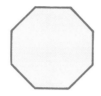

These polygons are all octagons. They all have the same
shape and they are all the same size. We say that they are
congruent.
Which of these pairs of polygons are congruent?
(You may need to trace one of each pair of polygons, cut
it out, and try to fit it to the other polygon.)

1.

2.

3.

4.

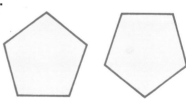

5.

6.

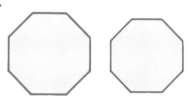

Trace these triangles and cut them out. For each one, cut another triangle that is congruent to it.

Take each pair of congruent triangles and fit them together to form another polygon. Name the polygon that you form. (Perhaps you can make more than one with each pair.)

Solid figures

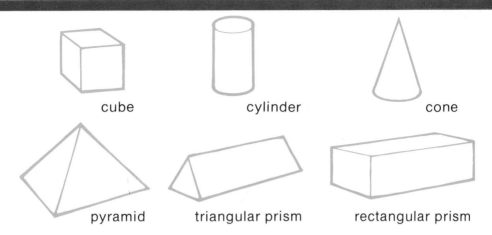

cube   cylinder   cone

pyramid   triangular prism   rectangular prism

These are called **solid figures**.
Write the names of these solids across your paper. Below each write the number of the object that is most like that solid.

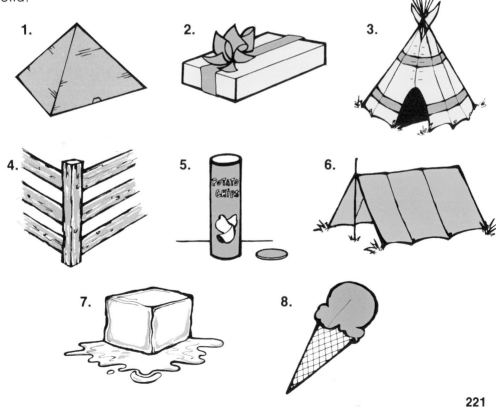

1.

2.

3.

4.

5.

6.

7.

8.

The **volume** of a solid is measured in **cubic units**.

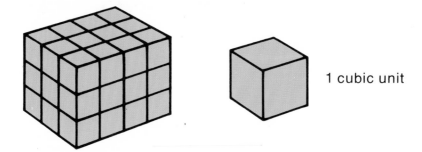

1 cubic unit

Imagine that you are filling this box with cubes.

a. You can put a row of 4 cubes along one side of the box.

b. There is room for 3 rows of 4 cubes each, so there are 12 cubes in the bottom layer.

c. There is room for 3 layers of cubes, so you know the box holds 36 cubes altogether.

The volume of the box is 36 cubic units.

Answer these questions for each box.

a. How many cubic units can be put in one row?

b. How many rows of cubic units are in the bottom layer?

c. How many cubic units are in the bottom layer altogether?

d. How many layers are there?

e. How many cubic units are needed to fill the box?

1.   **2.**   **3.**   **4.**

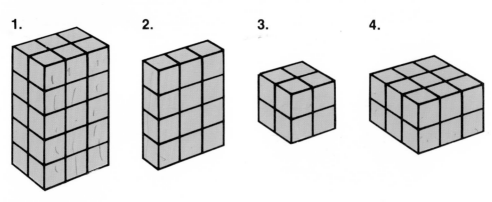

Comparing volumes

Which has the greater volume?

	A.	**B.**
1.	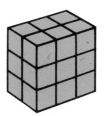	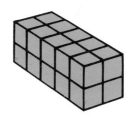
2.	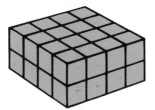	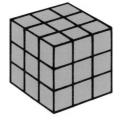
3.	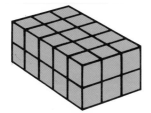	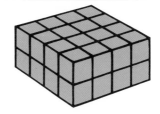
4.		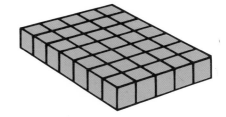
5.	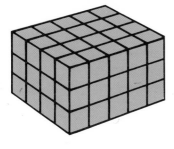	

223

You are already familiar with the idea of **symmetry**. If you are careful to observe the world about you, you will see many examples of symmetry.

Do you know why these illustrations are said to be symmetrical? Can you imagine a line through the middle of each figure that separates it into two parts?

What can you say about the two parts?
Are they exactly alike?
Are they almost alike?

Sometimes the best way to learn about something is to experiment. There are experiments about symmetry on the following pages that should help you answer the questions above.

Symmetry experiments

You will need these materials for your experiments:

    sheets of plain white paper
    drawing compass (or a lid to draw around)
    scissors
    ruler or straightedge
    mirror
    crayons or colored pencils

Experiment A
1. Draw a circle. You may call it the moon.
2. Draw a line segment through the center of the moon with the ruler.
3. Color one-half of the moon yellow.
4. Place the mirror so that the half-moon becomes a whole moon. (If you want a face on your moon, draw one eye and half a mouth. Perhaps you will want a nose also.)

Experiment B
1. Draw a shape like a splatter of paint.
2. Color it blue or black.
3. Place the mirror to make the shape appear larger.
4. Place the mirror to make the shape appear smaller.
5. Place the mirror to make the shape disappear.

Experiment C
1. Place your left hand flat on your desk.
2. Place the mirror near your fingertips.
   Do you see a right or a left hand in the mirror?
3. Repeat the activity with the right hand.
   Do you see a right or a left hand in the mirror?

Experiment D
1. Draw a heart on a sheet of paper.
   Does it look right?
2. Use a mirror to make it look better.
   Why does it look better when you place the mirror at the middle?

Experiment E
1. Fold a sheet of paper in half.
2. On the fold, draw half a heart.
3. Cut it out.
4. Unfold the heart. Do you like the way it looks?
5. Color the heart red.
6. Place your mirror on the line where the heart was folded.
   Do you think both parts of the heart are exactly the same size and shape? Try this to see.
7. Cut the heart along the fold line.
8. Keep the red side of both pieces facing up and place one piece on top of the other.
   Do you think both parts of the heart are the same size and shape? What do you have to do to make the two pieces fit one on top of the other?
9. Try some other cut-outs from the piece of folded paper. You may wish to make an airplane, a butterfly, or a tree.

   Can you see that each shape you cut from the folded paper will be symmetrical?

Experiment F

1. Look at yourself in the mirror. What you see is your *image.*
2. Place the edge of the mirror against the nose and forehead of a friend. Does it seem as if you can see his whole face?
   We know that our faces are like the face you made in the moon. We say that they have *symmetry* or that they are symmetrical. Use your mirror to check the five pictures on page 224. Try to find the line that separates each object into two parts. This line is called the *line of symmetry*.
   Now you are ready for a definition of the word *symmetry:*

   An object or figure has symmetry if each half is a mirror image of the other half.

1. Match.

    a. line
    b. ray
    c. perpendicular lines
    d. parallel lines
    e. line segment

1. 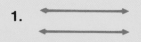   **2.**

3. 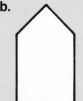   **4.**

5. 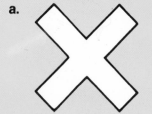   **6.**

2. Fill in the blanks.

    a. Volume is measured in _____ units.
    b. Area is measured in _____ units.
    c. The point where two lines cross is called the point of _____ .

3. Explain how a figure can be both a square and a rectangle at the same time.

4. Find the area of this region.   **5.** Find the volume of this solid.

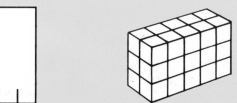

6. Which of these have at least one line of symmetry?

  a.   **b.**   **c.**

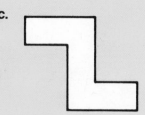

You can make curves from line segments.

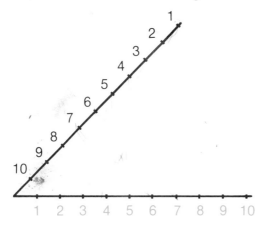

Trace this angle. Copy the numbers.

Connect the orange 1 with the black 1, the orange 2 with the black 2, etc., until each pair of numbers has been connected.

Unit 8

Casey Jones

Casey Jones, the famous engineer, was a credit to the good name he shared with his cousin, the evangelist Sam Jones. In fact, Casey had only one serious flaw: he sometimes forgot or ignored the seemingly unimportant rules of the railroads. Although he was never in serious trouble, nine times he was called down about breaking these rules. Because he had not made a habit of obeying all the rules, some people still blame him for what happened on April 30, 1900.

When Casey picked up the Cannonball at Memphis early that Monday morning, it was ninety minutes late. The night had been wet, but the track was clear, and Casey and his fireman, Sim Webb, were eager to roll. Casey took the controls and Sim managed the great boiler as the engine not only made its scheduled speed, but also caught up 88 minutes of its late time. Casey guided the speeding engine over the curves, grades, and bridges that made up the track south of Memphis. Suddenly, just north of Vaughn, Mississippi, Sim and Casey saw the two red lights of a train stopped in the track ahead of them. Casey told Sim to jump. He tried to stop the speeding train but failed. The Cannonball crashed into the back of the stopped freight train. Casey Jones died that night. He was the only fatality of the only serious wreck he was ever in.

The investigation afterward produced conflicting stories. The crew of the stopped train said that they had set the proper signals about half a mile behind their train but that Casey had ignored them. Casey's crew said that there were no signals. Only Casey knew the truth.

The investigators finally determined that Casey's record of little mistakes indicated that he was probably to blame. Today no one is sure. The great Casey Jones may have been innocent, but history will blame him for the wreck because of the nine little rules he had broken before. This man with a nearly perfect record was found guilty because he was not faithful in little things. (See Luke 16:10.)

Goals for Unit 8

1. I will learn how to find a part of a set.
2. I will learn how to find the average of several amounts.
3. I will learn to use ratios to help me solve problems.
4. I will be able to help myself solve story problems.
5. I will learn to divide by a two-digit divisor.

Words to Remember

average
ratio

1. Write a story problem that would be solved by this equation: $38 \div 19 =$ _____ .

2. Jenny had sixteen marbles. Ten of them were white and six were colored. Jenny had how many more white marbles than colored ones?
   a. Make a drawing to show how to find the answer to this problem.
   b. Write an equation that would be used to solve this problem.

3. Tell what operation would be used to solve each of these problems.
   a. Jill had 45¢. How many apples could she buy if they cost 9¢ each?
   b. Tom had 36¢. He spent 28¢ to buy two candy bars. How much money did he have left?
   c. Sally has three skirts and four blouses. How many different combinations can she make from these articles of clothing?
   d. Sammy read three books each week for six weeks. Each book had more than one hundred pages in it. How many books did he read in all?

4. Write a story problem that would be solved by each of these equations.

   a. $50 \div 10 =$ _____
   b. $9 \times 15 =$ _____
   c. $36 - 24 =$ _____
   d. $9 + 6 + 18 =$ _____

5. What are some ways you help yourself solve story problems?

Chad has six cookies. He has decided to eat one-half of them today and save the other half of them for tomorrow. How many cookies will he eat each day?

$$\tfrac{1}{2} \text{ of } 6 = \underline{\hspace{2cm}}$$

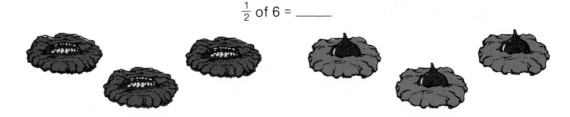

You can find $\tfrac{1}{2}$ of a set by dividing the set into two parts that are the same size. Look back to page 65. Do you remember that $\tfrac{6}{2}$ is a way to write "Six divided by two"? We often write the solution to the problem given above this way:

$$\tfrac{1}{2} \text{ of } 6 = \tfrac{6}{2} = 3$$

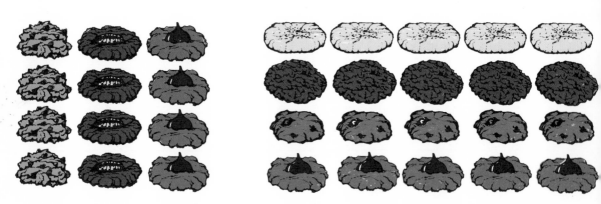

How could you find $\tfrac{1}{3}$ of a set of 12?

$$\tfrac{1}{3} \text{ of } 12 = \tfrac{12}{3} = ?$$

How could you find $\tfrac{1}{4}$ of a set of 20?

$$\tfrac{1}{4} \text{ of } 20 = \tfrac{20}{4} = ?$$

Solve these problems by dividing. Make a drawing to show that your answer is correct.

1. Maggie had twelve dolls. She gave one-fourth of them to her sister. How many dolls did she give away?

2. Jim had ten balls. One-fifth of them were baseballs. How many baseballs did he have?

3. Mother put fourteen cookies on a plate. Her children ate half of them. How many cookies did the children eat?

Solve these problems by dividing. Do not make a drawing.

4. Tommy solved twenty math problems. He got one-tenth of them wrong. How many problems did he get wrong?

5. There are twenty-seven students in Mrs. Clark's classroom. One-third of them are in grade three and the rest are in grade four. How many students are in grade three?

6. Mrs. Taylor bought thirty cookies. One-fifth of them were chocolate chip cookies. How many chocolate chip cookies did she buy?

7. Tina bought a package of fifteen balloons. She noticed that one-third of them were green. How many green balloons did she buy?

8. Joe's dog had eight puppies. One-half of them were all black. How many black puppies were there?

Solve these problems by making a drawing.

9. Greg's ball team played nine games. They won two-thirds of them. How many games did they win?

10. Kim read twelve books. Three-fourths of them were about animals. How many books about animals did Kim read?

1. Solve.

    a. $\frac{1}{3}$ of 9 =   **b.** $\frac{1}{6}$ of 24 =   **c.** $\frac{1}{8}$ of 64 =

    d. $\frac{1}{5}$ of 25 =   **e.** $\frac{1}{10}$ of 40 =   **f.** $\frac{1}{3}$ of 36 =

    g. $\frac{1}{2}$ of 18 =   **h.** $\frac{1}{7}$ of 28 =   **i.** $\frac{1}{4}$ of 32 =

    j. $\frac{1}{9}$ of 63 =   **k.** $\frac{1}{5}$ of 40 =   **l.** $\frac{1}{2}$ of 64 =

2. Write a story problem to go with each of these equations.

    a. $\frac{1}{2}$ of 18 = 9   **b.** $\frac{1}{5}$ of 25 = 5   **c.** $\frac{1}{3}$ of 9 = 3

Something for Fun

Give the name of each numbered shape used in the picture.

Finding averages

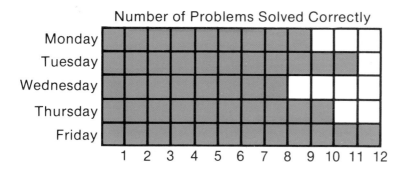

Number of Problems Solved Correctly

Monday												
Tuesday												
Wednesday												
Thursday												
Friday												

1 2 3 4 5 6 7 8 9 10 11 12

Mrs. Baker gave her class twelve math problems each day for a week. The students made graphs to show how many problems they solved correctly each day. This is Kathy's graph.

a. How many problems did Kathy solve correctly each of the days?

b. How many problems did Kathy solve correctly altogether?

Mrs. Baker explained to the class how to find the **average** number of problems they solved correctly each day. This is what Kathy did.

$$\begin{array}{r} 9 \\ 11 \\ 8 \\ 10 \\ +\ 12 \\ \hline 50 \end{array} \qquad \begin{array}{r} 10 \\ 5)\overline{50} \end{array}$$

Kathy correctly solved an average of ten problems each day.

c. How much above her average did Kathy score on Tuesday? How much above her average did she score on Friday?

d. How much below her average did Kathy score on Monday? How much below her average did she score on Wednesday?

e. Explain in your own words what the word *average* means.

1. These are the heights of four boys:

   | Eric | 70 centimeters | Dave | 75 centimeters |
   | Mark | 68 centimeters | Don | 71 centimeters |

   What is the average height of these boys?

2. These are Karen's piano practice times:

Monday	30 minutes	Thursday	25 minutes
Tuesday	30 minutes	Friday	35 minutes
Wednesday	40 minutes	Saturday	20 minutes

   She practiced an average of how many minutes each day?

3. These are the distances Mr. Bixler ran last week:

Monday	2 kilometers	Friday	3 kilometers
Tuesday	3 kilometers	Saturday	3 kilometers
Wednesday	0 kilometers	Sunday	0 kilometers
Thursday	3 kilometers		

   He ran an average of how many kilometers each day?

4. This chart shows the number of children in each of six families. What is the average number of children in those families?

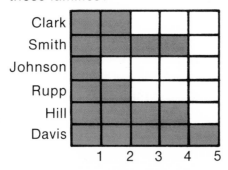

5. In four weeks Steve read a total of sixteen books. He read an average of how many books each week?

6. When the Steveson family went on their vacation, they drove an average of 236 miles each of the six days they were gone. How many miles did they drive altogether?

7. Mr. Miller has four collie dogs. Their weights are 70 pounds, 75 pounds, 82 pounds, and 73 pounds. What is the average weight of the dogs?

8. Mr. and Mrs. Cox and their two children went out to eat. The total cost of their meals was $11.36. What was the average cost of each meal?

Miss Rupp divided her class into teams. Each team had three girls and two boys on it.

You can write a pair of numbers to compare the number of girls and boys on each team. The pair of numbers is called a **ratio.**

> 3 to 2

Each person on Team A is able to do five division problems in two minutes.

We can write a ratio to tell that information.

> 5 to 2

Carla and Carol are twins but Carol works faster than Carla. Carol can do five multiplication problems in the same time that Carla can do three problems. What is the ratio that compares the number of problems that Carol can do to the number that Carla can do?

Write a ratio for each.

1. Mary can walk five blocks in nine minutes.
2. You can buy two pencils for 15¢.
3. Tim ran three miles in twenty-five minutes.
4. There are twelve red marbles and eight blue marbles in each package.
5. Mother scrambled seven eggs for four persons.

Mrs. Rogers makes grape punch by mixing two cups of grape juice with three cups of lemonade.

The ratio is 2 to 3.

If she used four cups of grape juice, she would use six cups of lemonade. This ratio is 4 to 6.

What is the ratio for this picture?

You can make a chart to show the number of cups of grape juice and lemonade needed to make the punch.

Cups of grape juice	2	4	6	8	10	12
Cups of lemonade	3	6	9	12	15	18

Mrs. Rogers is planning to make enough punch so that each of her thirty students can have at least one cupful. She plans to use twelve cups of grape juice.
   a. How many cups of lemonade will she use?
   b. How many cups of punch will she have altogether?
   c. Will there be enough for the class?

Using ratios to solve problems

You can use ratios to help you solve problems.

1. The price of three balloons is 19¢. How much will twelve balloons cost?

Balloons	3	6	9	12
Cost	19¢			

2. The art teacher decided that an art project can be done with four students sharing five sheets of paper. How many sheets of paper will be needed for a class of twenty-four students?

Students		4	8	12	16	20	24
Sheets of paper		5					

3. Three gumballs can be bought for 5¢. What will twelve gumballs cost?

Gumballs	3			
Cost	5¢			

4. Two lightbulbs cost 75¢. What is the cost of ten lightbulbs?

Lightbulbs	2				
Cost	75¢				

5. Mr. Spence mixes two parts peat moss and three parts garden soil to fill his flower boxes. If he uses eight pails of peat moss, how many pails of garden soil should he use?

Peat moss	2			
Garden soil	3			

241

Make charts of ratios to help you solve these problems.

1. You can buy three cupcakes for 25¢. How much will nine cupcakes cost?

Cupcakes	3	6	9
Cost	25¢		

2. A grocery store has a special price for cake mixes. The mixes are two for 75¢. What is the price of twelve boxes of cake mix?

3. A candy store was selling two ounces of fudge for 45¢. At this price, what is the cost of a pound of fudge?

4. A map is drawn so that three centimeters represents 100 kilometers. What distance would be represented by nine centimeters on the map?

5. Tim can ride his bike two miles in fifteen minutes. At this speed, how long will it take him to ride ten miles?

6. Mrs. Curtis uses a mixture of three oranges and two bananas when she makes fruit salad. How many bananas does she need when she uses twelve oranges?

7. Some students are making paper flower decorations. Each decoration is made of five leaves and three flowers. The students have made twenty-five leaves. How many flowers do they need to make?

8. A recipe for French toast says to mix three eggs with $\frac{1}{2}$ cup of milk. How many eggs will be needed when two cups of milk are used?

9. Bill's mother was making award ribbons for a track meet. She could make three awards out of each meter of ribbon she had. If she had three meters of ribbon, how many awards could she make?

10. Jim's father said that if he ran around the ballfield three times, he would have run two kilometers. Jim ran around the field fifteen times. How many kilometers did he run?

Equal ratios

Each student in Miss Rupp's class can solve three
division problems in two minutes. We can write the ratio
that shows this information in two ways:

3 to 2 or $\frac{3}{2}$ We read them both "Three to two."

Problems	3	6	9	12
Minutes	2	4	6	8

At that speed the class can do
6 problems in 4 minutes $\frac{6}{4}$
9 problems in 6 minutes $\frac{9}{6}$
12 problems in 8 minutes $\frac{12}{8}$

The ratios $\frac{3}{2}$, $\frac{6}{4}$, $\frac{9}{6}$, and $\frac{12}{8}$ are *equal ratios.*

Complete this chart of ratios.

Balloons	4	8	12
Cost	10¢		

a. How did you find the cost of eight balloons?
b. How did you find the cost of twelve balloons?

You can multiply to find equal ratios.

$$\frac{2 \times 4}{2 \times 10} = \frac{8}{20} \qquad \frac{4}{10} = \frac{8}{20} \qquad \frac{3 \times 4}{3 \times 10} = \frac{12}{30} \qquad \frac{4}{10} = \frac{12}{30}$$

Multiply both 4 and 10 by 2.   Multiply both 4 and 10 by 3.

c. Multiply to find the cost of sixteen balloons.
d. Multiply to find the cost of twenty balloons.

$$\frac{4 \times 4}{4 \times 10} = \frac{16}{?}$$

$$\frac{5 \times 4}{5 \times 10} = \frac{20}{?}$$

243

Finding equal ratios

1. 3 for 10¢
   What will 15 cost?

   $$\frac{\square \times 3}{\square \times 10} = \frac{15}{?}$$

   Multiply both 3 and 10 by what number?

2. 5 for $2
   What will 20 cost?

   $$\frac{\square \times 5}{\square \times 2} = \frac{20}{?}$$

   Multiply both 5 and 2 by what number?

3. 6 for $8
   What will 18 cost?

   $$\frac{\square \times 6}{\square \times 8} = \frac{18}{?}$$

   Multiply both 6 and 8 by what number?

4. 3 for 25¢
   What will 12 cost?

   $$\frac{\square \times 3}{\square \times 25} = \frac{12}{?}$$

   Multiply both 3 and 25 by what number?

5. 4 for $3
   What will 16 cost?

6. 2 for 15¢
   What will 8 cost?

7. 5 for 12¢
   What will 15 cost?

8. 2 for 59¢
   What will 6 cost?

9. 6 for 15¢
   What will 18 cost?

10. 3 for $1
    What will 12 cost?

Addition

One of the most important reasons that we study mathematics is that we need to be able to solve the problems we have as we live our lives every day. It is not enough to know *how* to add, subtract, multiply, and divide. We must also know *when* to use these operations.

Addition

Can you tell in your own words when we use the addition operation? (Look on page 16 for help if you need it.) Can you show with objects what happens when the addition operation is used?

Write an addition story problem for each of these equations. Solve them.

1. $8 + 6 + 3 =$ _____
2. $30 + 30 + 50 + 50 =$ _____
3. $\$1.59 + \$6.38 + \$0.14 =$ _____
4. $2,000 + 1,980 =$ _____

Did you use the words *total, in all,* or *altogether*? These words are often used in addition problems.

5. Millie read 18 books in January, 21 books in February, and 26 books in March. What was the total number of books she read in those three months?
6. There are 341 students in the elementary school, 108 students in the junior high, and 89 students in the high school at Westside Christian school. There are how many students in all at that school?
7. Mr. Craig worked 9 hours each day on Monday and Tuesday, 7 hours on Wednesday, 8 hours on Thursday, and 10 hours on Friday. How many hours did he work altogether that week?

Subtraction

The subtraction operation is used in at least four different situations.

> **1.** Taking away
> **2.** Comparing
> **3.** Finding a missing addend
> **4.** Finding a part

Can you tell in your own words when to use each of these kinds of subtraction? (Look on pages 17, 18, 19, and 20 for help if you need it.)

Can you show with objects what happens with each of these kinds of subtraction?

Write a story problem for each of these equations. Use the kind of subtraction that is asked for.

1. $0.75 - $0.38 = _____ (taking away)
2. 18 - 9 = _____ (comparing)
3. $27 - $18 = _____ (finding the missing addend)
4. 500 - 276 = _____ (finding a part of the whole)

Did you use the words *how many left, how many more,* or *how many fewer* in your problems? These words are often used in subtraction problems.

Solve. Tell which kind of subtraction is used in each problem.

5. Tony is reading a book that has 216 pages. He has read 139 pages so far. How many pages are left to read?
6. Ralph ran 38 miles one month. His father ran 76 miles that same month. Ralph ran how many fewer miles than his father?
7. Miss Crane's class set a goal of collecting $50 for a missionary family. So far they have $32. How much more do they need to collect?

Solving problems

Solve these problems.

1. Millie had 34 kinds of seeds in her seed collection. She had 26 kinds of fruit and vegetable seeds and the rest were flower seeds. How many kinds of flower seeds did she have?

2. Eric had $1.36 in his billfold and $3.75 in his bank. Did he have enough money to buy a model car kit that cost $5.00?

3. Mrs. Davis spent $3.95 for a book. She had $6.05 left. How much money did she have to start with?

4. There are 314 students in the elementary school and 174 students in the high school. How many more elementary students are there?

5. Miss Carson's class set a goal of 500 miles in their "Run for Fun" project. So far they have run a total of 262 miles. How many more miles do they need to run to reach their goal?

6. Janice has read 36 books this year. Jeff has read 17 more books than Janice. How many books has Jeff read?

7. The tallest student in Miss Carson's class is 130 centimeters tall. The shortest student is 115 centimeters tall. What is the difference between their heights?

8. Carey counted the sheets of art paper in the supply closet. There were 39 sheets of blue, 7 sheets of green, 53 sheets of yellow, 24 sheets of red, and 1 full package of 100 sheets of black. How many sheets of art paper were there altogether?

9. Write a story problem for each of these equations.

   a. $36 + 24 + 30 = $ _____

   b. $75 - 60 = $ _____   (Tell what kind of subtraction is needed to solve your problem.)

Multiplication

There are at least two kinds of situations for which we use the multiplication operation.

1. A shortcut for addition
2. Finding a cross product

Can you tell in your own words when to use each of these kinds of multiplication? (Look on pages 44 and 53 for help if you need it.)

Can you show with objects what happens in each kind of multiplication?

Write a story problem for each of these equations. Use the kind of multiplication that is asked for.

1. 3 × 42 = _____ (shortcut for addition)
2. 3 × 4 = _____ (finding cross products)
3. 12 × 36 = _____ (shortcut for addition)
4. 5 × $1.36 = _____ (shortcut for addition)

Did you use the words *total, in all,* or *altogether* in your problems for numbers 1, 3, and 4? Why can you use the same words you used in addition problems? When you see these words in a problem, how do you know whether to add or multiply?

Solve.

5. The principal said he had bought 25 new books for each of the 15 classrooms in the elementary school. How many books did he buy altogether?
6. The lunchroom provided four kinds of sandwiches and three kinds of drink. How many different combinations of a sandwich and a drink were possible?
7. Mrs. Baker bought five pounds of potatoes. They cost $0.17 a pound. What was the total cost?

The division operation is used in two different situations.

1. Finding how many sets of a given size can be made
2. Finding how many objects will be in each of a given number of sets

Can you explain in your own words how these situations are different? (Look on page 64 for help if you need it.)

Can you show with objects what happens in each of these kinds of division?

Write a story problem for each of these equations. Use the kind of division that is asked for.

1. $36 \div 4 =$ _____ (find how many sets can be made)
2. $164 \div 2 =$ _____ (find how many in each set)
3. $75 \div 5 =$ _____ (find how many in each set)
4. $386 \div 9 =$ _____ (find how many in each set)

Solve. Tell whether the problem is like the first or the second kind that is given at the top of the page.

5. Billie bought eight pounds of apples. She paid $1.76. What was the price of one pound?
6. Mrs. Turner had 72 sheets of construction paper. She asked Troy to put 3 sheets on each student's desk. There was enough for how many desks?
7. There were 36 children at a party. One game needed teams of 3 children each. How many teams could be formed?

1. A class was making bookmarks to give to their mothers for Mother's Day. Eight inches of ribbon was needed for each bookmark. The teacher had a roll of ribbon that was 178 inches long.
   a. How many bookmarks could be made?
   b. How many inches of ribbon would be left?
   c. What would be the sensible thing to do with the remainder?
2. There are 46 children on the playground. The teacher formed 4 teams with the same number of children on each team.
   a. How many children were on each team?
   b. How many extra children were there?
   c. What would be the sensible thing to do with the remaining children?
3. Mrs. Simm's class of 27 students is going on a field trip. Five students can ride in each car.
   a. How many cars are needed?
   b. Will there be five students in each car?

Solve each problem. Decide what is the sensible thing to do with the remainders.

1. Tonya is helping her father in their store. They are putting 8 packages of candles into large boxes. How many boxes are needed for 277 packages?

2. Each table in the lunchroom is large enough to seat eight persons. There are 100 persons coming to a banquet. How many tables will be needed?

3. A store is selling cans of tomatoes at a price of two cans for 59¢. How much will one can of tomatoes cost?

4. A lollipop costs 6¢. Sharon has 25¢. How many lollipops can she buy?

5. A carpenter has a board that is 6 feet long. He needs pieces of wood that are 7 inches long. How many pieces of wood that are 7 inches long can he cut from the board?

Do you remember these ways of helping yourself solve
story problems?

> **1.** Read it aloud.
> **2.** Draw a picture.
> **3.** Draw a number line.
> **4.** Make a chart.

Use one or more of these suggestions to help you solve
these problems.

1. The playground at Faith Christian School is shaped
   like a rectangle. It is 480 feet long and 180 feet wide.
   Tim ran all the way around the playground two times
   one day. How many feet did he run?
2. There were 28 students in Miss Lint's class. Nineteen
   of these students were boys. There were how many
   more boys than girls in this class?
3. Miss Lint asked her students to learn five Bible
   questions and answers each week. How many weeks
   will it take to learn 150 questions and answers?
4. A bulletin board in the classroom is four feet long
   and three feet wide. What is the area of this bulletin
   board?
5. Miss Lint's class had a pizza party. They decided that
   one pizza would serve four students. How many
   pizzas were needed for the whole class of 28
   students?
6. One day in math class Miss Lint timed the students as
   they worked. Tony and Lisa each solved five problems
   in three minutes. At that speed, how many problems
   could they solve in fifteen minutes?
7. The music class started at 12:45 and lasted 45
   minutes. At what time did the music class end?
8. One day the lunchroom menu showed that the
   students could choose a tuna sandwich, a cheese
   sandwich, or a ham sandwich. They could also
   choose orange juice or milk to drink. How many
   different combinations were possible if a student took
   one sandwich and one drink?

How To Solve Problems
1. Read to find the question.
2. Read to find the information.
3. Decide what to do.
4. Figure out the answer.
5. Decide if the answer makes sense.

Some students have trouble solving story problems because they do not read them carefully. Do you remember to use suggestions like these to help you when you solve problems?

Solve.

1. Mrs. Clark planted three rows of onions in her garden. She put thirty onions in each row. How many onions did she plant?

2. Mrs. Clark had eighteen tomato plants. She put nine plants in each row. How many rows of tomatoes did she have?

3. There was room in the garden for six rows of corn. Each row was thirty feet long. What was the total length of the rows of corn?

4. One package of lettuce seed has enough seed to plant a row twenty-five feet long. Mrs. Clark has three packages. How many feet of lettuce can she plant?

5. Mrs. Clark planted three rows of green beans and two rows of yellow beans. Each row was thirty feet long. What was the total length of the bean rows?

6. Mrs. Clark bought three containers of pepper plants. Each had six plants in it. She gave four of the plants to her neighbor. How many pepper plants did Mrs. Clark have left?

7. The garden is thirty feet long and twenty feet wide. How many feet of fence are needed to go all the way around the garden?

8. During the summer Mrs. Clark froze thirty-two packages of yellow beans and eighteen packages of green beans. She froze how many more packages of yellow beans than green ones?

9. Mrs. Clark harvested a total of 130 pounds of tomatoes. She gave 25 pounds of them to her friends. How many pounds of tomatoes did she keep for her family?

10. Mrs. Clark put eight ears of corn in each package that she froze. During the summer she froze 268 ears of corn. How many packages did she have?

11. Six of the pepper plants had fourteen peppers each. If peppers cost ten cents each in a store, what was the value of the peppers grown on these six plants?

12. Mrs. Clark paid her son Jeff seventy-five cents an hour to help her in the garden. He worked five hours in May, eight hours in June, nine hours in July, and ten hours in August.

  a. Jeff worked an average of how many hours each month?

  b. How much did Jeff earn altogether?

This is a page from Margaret's record book.

May			Income	Outgo
	From April		$ 1.38	
1	Allowance		0.35	
1		Savings		$ 0.05
3		Sunday School		0.05
8	Allowance		0.35	
8		Savings		0.05
9		Flower for Mother		1.25
10		Sunday School		0.05
15	Allowance		0.35	
15		Savings		0.05
16	Raking lawns		2.00	
		Savings		0.50
17		Sunday School		0.25
18		Book		1.12
22	Allowance		0.35	
22		Savings		0.05
24		Sunday School		0.05
28	Helping in garden		0.50	
29	Allowance		0.35	
29		Savings		0.05
31		Sunday School		0.10

1. What was the total amount of Margaret's allowance for the month of May?
2. How much did Margaret save during May?
3. How much did Margaret give in Sunday School that month? Why do you think she gave $0.25 on May 17 instead of $0.05 like she gave on May 3 and May 10?
4. How much did Margaret receive altogether during May?
5. How much money did Margaret have on June 1?

Buying groceries

When a missionary goes grocery shopping, she often finds that the prices are quite different from what they are at home. In February, 1980, Miss Hager in Puerto Rico and Miss Jones in the Dominican Republic each made a list of some prices they paid. Notice that many of the items cost more in those places than they did in South Carolina at the same time.

Item	Puerto Rico	Dominican Republic	South Carolina
5 lb. sugar	$1.92	$0.75	$1.79
5 lb. flour	1.33	0.84	0.89
1 lb. coffee	3.87	4.58	2.89
1 doz. eggs	1.35	0.88	0.69
1 qt. mayonnaise	2.19	3.09	1.19
3 lb. shortening	3.23	4.83	1.79
1 can pears	1.19	1.67	0.89
1 loaf bread	0.75	0.38	0.63
1 cake mix	1.31	1.67	0.59
1 lb. ground beef	2.59	1.30	1.29
1 lb. pork chops	2.59	1.30	1.29
1 qt. milk	0.57	0.38	0.61
1 head of lettuce	1.00	0.30	0.33
12 oz. peanut butter	1.13	1.62	1.15
12 oz. cereal	1.43	1.00	1.15

Imagine that you are buying groceries in each of these places. Find the total cost for each list in each place.

Where would these groceries cost the most?

1 lb. coffee
3 doz. eggs
2 cake mixes
2 heads of lettuce
3 qt. milk
3 lb. pork chops

Where would these groceries cost the most?

3 loaves bread
2 lb. ground beef
1 lb. coffee
12 oz. cereal
3 lb. shortening
5 lb. flour

Where would these groceries cost the most?

2 qt. milk
5 lb. flour
5 lb. sugar
3 lb. ground beef
1 head of lettuce
12 oz. peanut butter

Longest rivers in North America	
Mackenzie	2,635 miles
Missouri	2,466
Mississippi	2,348
St. Lawrence	1,900
Rio Grande	1,885
Yukon	1,800
Arkansas	1,450
Colorado	1,450
Columbia	1,214

Longest rivers in the world	
Nile (Africa)	4,132 miles
Amazon (S. America)	3,900
Yangtze (Asia)	3,430
Hwang Ho (Asia)	2,903
Congo (Africa)	2,900
Amur (Asia)	2,802
Lena (Asia)	2,653
Mackenzie (N. America)	2,635
Mekong (Asia)	2,600
Niger (Africa)	2,590

1. The Rio Grande and the Colorado rivers are both in the southwestern United States. The Rio Grande is how many miles longer than the Colorado?
2. The Mackenzie river is in northern Canada. The Yukon river is in Alaska. Which river is longer? How much longer is it?
3. Can you find the Mississippi and the Missouri rivers on a map? The Missouri is how much longer than the Mississippi?
4. What is the total length of the Nile, the Congo, and the Niger rivers? On what continent are these rivers located?
5. Five rivers on the chart are located in Asia. What is their total length?
6. The longest river in South America is how much longer than the longest river in North America?

Patterns in division

1. Give the quotients aloud.

a. $1\overline{)2}$ $10\overline{)20}$ $100\overline{)200}$

b. $1\overline{)9}$ $10\overline{)90}$ $100\overline{)900}$

c. $2\overline{)8}$ $20\overline{)80}$ $200\overline{)800}$

d. $5\overline{)25}$ $50\overline{)250}$ $500\overline{)2,500}$

e. $5\overline{)40}$ $50\overline{)400}$ $500\overline{)4,000}$

2. Solve.

a. $500 \div 100 =$ b. $160 \div 40 =$ c. $240 \div 60 =$

d. $2500 \div 500 =$ e. $180 \div 30 =$ f. $210 \div 70 =$

g. $720 \div 80 =$ h. $3200 \div 800 =$ i. $450 \div 90 =$

j. $2000 \div 400 =$ k. $4200 \div 600 =$ l. $80 \div 40 =$

3. Copy and solve. Example:

$$\begin{array}{r} 4 \\ 40\overline{)165} \\ -\ 160 \\ \hline 5\ r \end{array}$$

a. $30\overline{)93}$ b. $20\overline{)107}$ c. $60\overline{)120}$ d. $40\overline{)250}$

e. $50\overline{)162}$ f. $60\overline{)188}$ g. $90\overline{)450}$ h. $20\overline{)196}$

i. $200\overline{)800}$ j. $500\overline{)3500}$ k. $800\overline{)1610}$ l. $300\overline{)915}$

Chet and Susan are helping in their father's store. They are putting empty bottles in cases. Each case holds 24 bottles. How many cases can be filled with 205 bottles? How many bottles will be left?

$$205 \div 24 = \underline{\hspace{2cm}}$$

This chart will help you find the answer.

$$
\begin{array}{r}
8 \\
24\overline{)205} \\
-192 \\
\hline
13r
\end{array}
$$

1 × 24 = 24	
2 × 24 = 48	
3 × 24 = 72	
4 × 24 = 96	
5 × 24 = 120	
6 × 24 = 144	
7 × 24 = 168	
8 × 24 = 192	
9 × 24 = 216	
10 × 24 = 240	

They can fill eight cases. There will be thirteen bottles left.

Use the charts to help you solve these problems.

1. $24\overline{)165}$ 2. $35\overline{)268}$ 3. $72\overline{)590}$

4. $35\overline{)290}$ 5. $24\overline{)200}$ 6. $35\overline{)185}$

7. $72\overline{)515}$ 8. $72\overline{)406}$ 9. $24\overline{)115}$

10. $35\overline{)216}$ 11. $72\overline{)600}$ 12. $24\overline{)153}$

1 × 35 = 35	
2 × 35 = 70	
3 × 35 = 105	
4 × 35 = 140	
5 × 35 = 175	
6 × 35 = 210	
7 × 35 = 245	
8 × 35 = 280	
9 × 35 = 315	
10 × 35 = 350	

1 × 72 = 72	
2 × 72 = 144	
3 × 72 = 216	
4 × 72 = 288	
5 × 72 = 360	
6 × 72 = 432	
7 × 72 = 504	
8 × 72 = 576	
9 × 72 = 648	
10 × 72 = 720	

Estimating quotients

You can find the quotient for these problems without using a multiplication chart. Round the divisor to the nearest 10 and estimate.

$22\overline{)138}$

How many 20s are in 138?
The answer is probably 6 because 6 × 20 = 120.

$$\begin{array}{r} 6 \\ 22\overline{)138} \\ -132 \\ \hline 6r \end{array}$$

$39\overline{)178}$

How many 40s are in 178?
The answer is probably 4 because 4 × 40 = 160.

$$\begin{array}{r} 4 \\ 39\overline{)178} \\ -156 \\ \hline 22r \end{array}$$

$73\overline{)593}$

How many 70s are in 593?
The answer is probably 8 because 8 × 70 = 560.

$$\begin{array}{r} 8 \\ 73\overline{)593} \\ -584 \\ \hline 9r \end{array}$$

Solve these problems.
Round the divisor to the nearest 10 and estimate.

1. $51\overline{)432}$ 2. $68\overline{)325}$ 3. $52\overline{)490}$ 4. $42\overline{)356}$

5. $79\overline{)612}$ 6. $82\overline{)504}$ 7. $32\overline{)166}$ 8. $47\overline{)253}$

9. $53\overline{)236}$ 10. $83\overline{)686}$ 11. $58\overline{)374}$ 12. $99\overline{)846}$

More estimating quotients

Sometimes when you round the divisor to the nearest 10
and estimate, your answer is not correct.

$15\overline{)65}$

How many 20s are in 65?

The answer is probably 3
because 3 × 20 = 60.

$$15\overline{)65} \quad \overset{3}{\phantom{15\overline{)65}}}$$

$\begin{array}{r} 3 \\ 15\overline{)65} \\ -45 \\ \hline 20 \end{array}$

$\begin{array}{r} 4 \\ 15\overline{)65} \\ -60 \\ \hline 5r \end{array}$

How do you know that 3 is not the correct quotient?

$73\overline{)562}$

How many 70s are in 562?

The answer is probably 8
because 8 × 70 = 560.

$\begin{array}{r} 8 \\ 73\overline{)562} \\ -584 \end{array}$

$\begin{array}{r} 7 \\ 73\overline{)562} \\ -511 \\ \hline 51r \end{array}$

How do you know that 8 is not the correct quotient?

Estimate. Solve the problem. If your first estimate is
incorrect, erase your work and try again.

1. 346 ÷ 58 =

2. 123 ÷ 32 =

3. 624 ÷ 78 =

4. 712 ÷ 85 =

5. 164 ÷ 18 =

6. 322 ÷ 65 =

7. 315 ÷ 43 =

8. 522 ÷ 88 =

9. 615 ÷ 43 =

10. 212 ÷ 31 =

11. 580 ÷ 76 =

12. 456 ÷ 82 =

Solve.

1. a. 349 ÷ 79 =   **2. a.** 264 ÷ 37 =   **3. a.** 158 ÷ 63 =   **4. a.** 426 ÷ 79 =
  b. 273 ÷ 61 =   **b.** 638 ÷ 72 =   **b.** 236 ÷ 29 =   **b.** 285 ÷ 66 =
  c. 641 ÷ 89 =   **c.** 513 ÷ 82 =   **c.** 418 ÷ 77 =   **c.** 316 ÷ 28 =
  d. 179 ÷ 37 =   **d.** 215 ÷ 90 =   **d.** 520 ÷ 48 =   **d.** 163 ÷ 23 =
  e. 623 ÷ 92 =   **e.** 763 ÷ 82 =   **e.** 250 ÷ 50 =   **e.** 416 ÷ 58 =
  f. 453 ÷ 58 =   **f.** 387 ÷ 67 =   **f.** 193 ÷ 26 =   **f.** 743 ÷ 82 =
  g. 510 ÷ 69 =   **g.** 431 ÷ 52 =   **g.** 487 ÷ 93 =   **g.** 500 ÷ 75 =
  h. 395 ÷ 42 =   **h.** 111 ÷ 34 =   **h.** 279 ÷ 61 =   **h.** 352 ÷ 64 =
  i. 166 ÷ 28 =   **i.** 268 ÷ 49 =   **i.** 700 ÷ 88 =   **i.** 195 ÷ 25 =
  j. 402 ÷ 58 =   **j.** 410 ÷ 80 =   **j.** 335 ÷ 56 =   **j.** 366 ÷ 51 =

1. Solve.

   a. $\frac{1}{3}$ of 15 =   **b.** $\frac{1}{5}$ of 25 =   **c.** $\frac{1}{4}$ of 24 =

2. Tom kept a record of how many spelling words he missed each week for six weeks.

   Week 1—missed 2 words   Week 4—missed 1 word
   Week 2—missed 4 words   Week 5—missed 3 words
   Week 3—missed 0 words   Week 6—missed 2 words

   Tom missed an average of how many words each week?

3. Make a ratio chart to solve this problem.
   You can buy two apples for 15¢. What is the cost of eight apples?

4. Write a pair of equal ratios to solve this problem.
   Ruth can solve five division problems in three minutes. At that speed, how long will it take her to solve fifteen problems?

5. Find the quotients.

   a. $36\overline{)256}$ **b.** $52\overline{)345}$ **c.** $18\overline{)128}$

6. Solve these problems.
   a. Miss Jones has eighty library books in her room. One-eighth of them are about horses. How many of those books are about horses?
   b. Bob noticed that six of the books each had 262 pages in them. These books have a total of how many pages?
   c. Miss Jones asked Terry to put the eighty books on four shelves with the same number of books on each shelf. How many books will be on each shelf?
   d. Joy decided to read five books each week until she had read all eighty of the books. How many weeks will it take her to finish reading all the books?
   e. Miss Jones noticed on Friday that there was a total of twenty-seven books checked out. How many books should have been on the shelves?
   f. Brent decided to read three books every two weeks. How many weeks will it take him to read fifteen books?

Number Puzzles

1. Fill in the missing signs (+ , - , × , or ÷).
Do the operations in order from left to right and from
top to bottom.

6		3		5	=	8
3		6		1	=	8
3		6		3	=	3
=		=		=		=
1		3		1	=	4

4		3		6	=	6
10		2		1	=	4
2		3		5	=	10
=		=		=		=
7		9		2	=	14

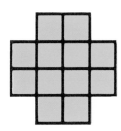

2. Arrange the numbers 1 through 12 in a
double cross so that the total amount in
each four-digit row and column is 26.

3. Mr. Kent needed six gallons of water.
He had only a two-gallon pail and a
five-gallon pail. How could he get just
six gallons? Can you think of more
than one way?

Practice

Addition with renaming of ones

1.

a. 36 27 + 14	**b.** 49 23 + 15	**c.** 12 68 + 19	**d.** 48 27 + 18	**e.** 36 19 + 43	**f.** 28 36 + 27
g. 26 32 + 19	**h.** 48 18 + 26	**i.** 39 29 + 27	**j.** 46 17 + 28	**k.** 28 26 + 35	**l.** 49 17 + 25

2.

a. 45 19 + 27	**b.** 36 29 + 38	**c.** 25 29 + 37	**d.** 19 27 + 48	**e.** 28 15 + 37	**f.** 36 28 + 19
g. 38 19 + 24	**h.** 45 18 + 29	**i.** 46 18 + 27	**j.** 48 17 + 28	**k.** 39 29 + 16	**l.** 27 38 + 27

Addition with renaming of tens and ones

1.

a. 126 328 + 174	**b.** 482 279 + 187	**c.** 284 199 + 387	**d.** 295 183 + 198	**e.** 628 173 + 159	**f.** 178 398 + 157
g. 275 349 + 194	**h.** 489 178 + 266	**i.** 356 288 + 298	**j.** 379 187 + 268	**k.** 487 198 + 286	**l.** 359 188 + 397

2.

a. 278	**b.** 158	**c.** 419	**d.** 390	**e.** 539	**f.** 458
409	327	287	287	187	268
+ 288	+ 490	+ 196	+ 169	+ 198	+ 192

g. 389	**h.** 498	**i.** 186	**j.** 523	**k.** 188	**l.** 404
295	176	319	198	297	268
+ 119	+ 199	+ 478	+ 209	+ 269	+ 119

Addition with renaming in any place

1.

a. 1,629	**b.** 5,629	**c.** 3,762	**d.** 7,358	**e.** 4,876
2,856	3,487	5,894	2,987	1,592
3,172	1,958	2,657	1,425	4,983
+ 9,584	+ 2,692	+ 4,829	+ 2,698	+ 2,799

f. 8,495	**g.** 9,787	**h.** 5,824	**i.** 4,927	**j.** 7,958
6,387	2,908	3,297	3,089	3,495
2,694	3,767	6,548	2,635	8,278
+ 3,879	+ 4,823	+ 3,295	+ 5,986	+ 6,695

2.

a. 654 + 8,936 + 95 + 723 =

b. 48 + 7,600 + 256 + 149 =

c. 3,654 + 82 + 954 + 687 =

d. 929 + 63 + 478 + 2,142 =

e. 36 + 7,293 + 865 + 18 =

f. 495 + 873 + 5,682 + 7 =

g. 3,487 + 792 + 82 + 736 =

h. 4,928 + 635 + 274 + 9 =

Subtraction with renaming of ten

1.

  a.   63   **b.**   52   **c.**   72   **d.**   53   **e.**   62   **f.**   40
   - 19   - 38   - 16   - 48   - 37   - 18

  g.   32   **h.**   41   **i.**   65   **j.**   72   **k.**   43   **l.**   62
   - 18   - 23   - 38   - 36   - 18   - 27

2.

  a.   93   **b.**   75   **c.**   32   **d.**   47   **e.**   52   **f.**   74
   - 18   - 26   - 18   - 39   - 28   - 48

  g.   51   **h.**   92   **i.**   71   **j.**   67   **k.**   95   **l.**   83
   - 37   - 86   - 38   - 58   - 79   - 29

Subtraction with renaming of a hundred

1.

  a.   328   **b.**   507   **c.**   618   **d.**   749   **e.**   427
   - 172   - 294   - 253   - 285   - 194

  f.   526   **g.**   714   **h.**   647   **i.**   915   **j.**   873
   - 183   - 280   - 195   - 372   - 192

2.

  a.   736   **b.**   544   **c.**   827   **d.**   924   **e.**   622
   - 285   - 370   - 653   - 672   - 142

  f.   525   **g.**   736   **h.**   428   **i.**   538   **j.**   927
   - 184   - 251   - 374   - 165   - 466

Subtraction with renaming of a ten and a hundred

1.

a. 536 - 387	**b.** 733 - 548	**c.** 435 - 169	**d.** 934 - 587	**e.** 827 - 369
f. 310 - 176	**g.** 523 - 279	**h.** 845 - 188	**i.** 414 - 267	**j.** 666 - 378

2.

a. 327 - 159	**b.** 536 - 288	**c.** 615 - 296	**d.** 723 - 394	**e.** 923 - 635
f. 828 - 179	**g.** 465 - 287	**h.** 437 - 299	**i.** 601 - 395	**j.** 835 - 189

Subtraction with renaming in any place

1.

a. 2,375 - 1,824	**b.** 6,132 - 1,495	**c.** 3,710 - 1,596	**d.** 8,215 - 4,682	**e.** 5,426 - 1,948
f. 4,256 - 1,768	**g.** 8,124 - 1,865	**h.** 3,920 - 1,687	**i.** 5,143 - 1,689	**j.** 7,111 - 2,630

2.

a. 2,138 - 1,895	**b.** 6,314 - 2,195	**c.** 3,264 - 982	**d.** 5,962 - 3,249	**e.** 7,456 - 2,929
f. 9,982 - 4,795	**g.** 1,826 - 954	**h.** 4,850 - 2,198	**i.** 9,261 - 5,938	**j.** 7,210 - 2,975

Subtraction with zeroes

1.

a. 200
   - 126

b. 600
   - 327

c. 400
   - 268

d. 300
   - 172

e. 800
   - 267

f. 600
   - 156

g. 900
   - 348

h. 700
   - 264

i. 900
   - 372

j. 400
   - 249

2.

a. 306
   - 195

b. 208
   - 169

c. 503
   - 476

d. 807
   - 299

e. 408
   - 278

f. 207
   - 158

g. 401
   - 275

h. 703
   - 384

i. 904
   - 167

j. 606
   - 248

3.

a. 2,000
   - 1,317

b. 5,000
   - 2,645

c. 8,000
   - 1,729

d. 4,000
   - 1,934

e. 6,000
   - 5,328

f. 10,000
   - 1,426

g. 7,000
   - 3,162

h. 9,000
   - 3,748

i. 6,000
   - 4,295

j. 10,000
   - 5,127

4.

a. 10,010
   - 1,426

b. 9,030
   - 5,729

c. 8,002
   - 4,695

d. 7,000
   - 3,857

e. 2,010
   - 1,784

f. 8,006
   - 1,568

g. 10,008
   - 1,769

h. 7,004
   - 1,395

i. 4,090
   - 1,837

j. 1,060
   - 387

5.

a. 2,000 - 1,568	**b.** 9,032 - 2,790	**c.** 5,006 - 2,847	**d.** 3,000 - 1,798	**e.** 5,060 - 3,927
f. 10,000 - 3,804	**g.** 10,005 - 1,728	**h.** 5,000 - 2,706	**i.** 8,080 - 2,936	**j.** 1,000 - 368

Multiplication with renaming of ones

1.

a. 25 × 3	**b.** 27 × 2	**c.** 47 × 2	**d.** 18 × 5	**e.** 38 × 2	**f.** 29 × 3
g. 15 × 6	**h.** 24 × 4	**i.** 37 × 2	**j.** 19 × 5	**k.** 39 × 2	**l.** 29 × 2

2.

a. 18 × 4	**b.** 26 × 3	**c.** 36 × 2	**d.** 19 × 4	**e.** 27 × 3	**f.** 48 × 2
g. 19 × 3	**h.** 13 × 7	**i.** 23 × 4	**j.** 14 × 6	**k.** 16 × 5	**l.** 17 × 3

Multiplication with renaming of ones and tens

1.

a. 126 × 8	**b.** 365 × 5	**c.** 473 × 7	**d.** 392 × 8	**e.** 166 × 9
f. 347 × 3	**g.** 588 × 5	**h.** 728 × 9	**i.** 374 × 7	**j.** 782 × 6

2.

a. 456 × 3	**b.** 827 × 8	**c.** 476 × 7	**d.** 289 × 9	**e.** 450 × 7
f. 768 × 4	**g.** 596 × 7	**h.** 327 × 8	**i.** 499 × 6	**j.** 572 × 8

3.

a. 197 × 3	**b.** 368 × 4	**c.** 817 × 5	**d.** 662 × 8	**e.** 498 × 6
f. 807 × 9	**g.** 487 × 4	**h.** 923 × 7	**i.** 358 × 8	**j.** 736 × 5

Multiplication by two-digit numbers

1.

a. 25 × 16	**b.** 38 × 24	**c.** 57 × 38	**d.** 45 × 29	**e.** 82 × 64
f. 73 × 46	**g.** 64 × 57	**h.** 32 × 88	**i.** 94 × 70	**j.** 39 × 57

2.

a.	86 × 27	b.	53 × 94	c.	72 × 86	d.	19 × 57	e.	30 × 45

f.	49 × 49	g.	84 × 63	h.	29 × 87	i.	35 × 90	j.	88 × 67

3.

a.	387 × 24	b.	192 × 65	c.	384 × 52	d.	904 × 78	e.	336 × 57

f.	295 × 76	g.	621 × 98	h.	375 × 48	i.	293 × 36	j.	448 × 65

4.

a.	107 × 74	b.	392 × 84	c.	467 × 56	d.	319 × 59	e.	176 × 25

f.	433 × 74	g.	816 × 29	h.	537 × 36	i.	598 × 43	j.	294 × 77

5.

a.	146 × 89	b.	350 × 47	c.	594 × 36	d.	841 × 19	e.	263 × 82

f.	940 × 82	g.	318 × 29	h.	775 × 27	i.	538 × 68	j.	398 × 45

Division

1. a. 75 ÷ 5 =   **2. a.** 91 ÷ 7 =
  b. 96 ÷ 8 =   **b.** 72 ÷ 3 =
  c. 76 ÷ 2 =   **c.** 96 ÷ 2 =
  d. 84 ÷ 3 =   **d.** 92 ÷ 4 =
  e. 85 ÷ 5 =   **e.** 68 ÷ 4 =
  f. 96 ÷ 6 =   **f.** 78 ÷ 2 =
  g. 72 ÷ 4 =   **g.** 90 ÷ 5 =
  h. 81 ÷ 3 =   **h.** 60 ÷ 4 =
  i. 96 ÷ 4 =   **i.** 84 ÷ 6 =
  j. 98 ÷ 7 =   **j.** 87 ÷ 3 =

3. a. 236 ÷ 4 =   **4. a.** 434 ÷ 7 =
  b. 135 ÷ 5 =   **b.** 498 ÷ 6 =
  c. 245 ÷ 5 =   **c.** 195 ÷ 3 =
  d. 390 ÷ 6 =   **d.** 364 ÷ 7 =
  e. 232 ÷ 4 =   **e.** 288 ÷ 9 =
  f. 174 ÷ 2 =   **f.** 216 ÷ 6 =
  g. 441 ÷ 9 =   **g.** 168 ÷ 3 =
  h. 564 ÷ 6 =   **h.** 415 ÷ 5 =
  i. 304 ÷ 4 =   **i.** 664 ÷ 8 =
  j. 335 ÷ 5 =   **j.** 588 ÷ 7 =

Division with remainders

1. a. 79 ÷ 3 =   **2. a.** 148 ÷ 5 =
  b. 86 ÷ 4 =   **b.** 265 ÷ 4 =
  c. 73 ÷ 5 =   **c.** 845 ÷ 3 =
  d. 98 ÷ 3 =   **d.** 178 ÷ 6 =
  e. 135 ÷ 4 =   **e.** 467 ÷ 9 =
  f. 93 ÷ 7 =   **f.** 364 ÷ 8 =
  g. 136 ÷ 9 =   **g.** 2,943 ÷ 7 =
  h. 192 ÷ 7 =   **h.** 1,928 ÷ 6 =
  i. 69 ÷ 5 =   **i.** 3,755 ÷ 9 =
  j. 346 ÷ 7 =   **j.** 2,326 ÷ 8 =

Division with zero in the quotient

1. a. 1,636 ÷ 4 =
   b. 2,500 ÷ 5 =
   c. 7,263 ÷ 9 =
   d. 7,208 ÷ 8 =
   e. 4,235 ÷ 7 =
   f. 624 ÷ 6 =
   g. 1,824 ÷ 6 =
   h. 5,624 ÷ 8 =
   i. 3,515 ÷ 5 =
   j. 4,536 ÷ 9 =

2. a. 3,017 ÷ 5 =
   b. 4,253 ÷ 6 =
   c. 4,926 ÷ 7 =
   d. 5,670 ÷ 8 =
   e. 3,048 ÷ 5 =
   f. 4,513 ÷ 9 =
   g. 1,627 ÷ 8 =
   h. 434 ÷ 4 =
   i. 9,100 ÷ 9 =
   j. 2,117 ÷ 2 =

Division by two-digit divisor

1. a. 265 ÷ 36 =
   b. 254 ÷ 42 =
   c. 92 ÷ 15 =
   d. 400 ÷ 52 =
   e. 156 ÷ 43 =
   f. 255 ÷ 27 =
   g. 853 ÷ 91 =
   h. 495 ÷ 57 =
   i. 175 ÷ 23 =
   j. 350 ÷ 45 =

2. a. 123 ÷ 25 =
   b. 280 ÷ 56 =
   c. 201 ÷ 81 =
   d. 348 ÷ 75 =
   e. 450 ÷ 89 =
   f. 295 ÷ 69 =
   g. 152 ÷ 24 =
   h. 418 ÷ 61 =
   i. 360 ÷ 64 =
   j. 472 ÷ 72 =

Renaming of fractions into lower terms

1.

a. $\frac{6}{8} =$ **b.** $\frac{3}{6} =$ **c.** $\frac{12}{14} =$ **d.** $\frac{8}{10} =$ **e.** $\frac{4}{6} =$ **f.** $\frac{3}{9} =$

g. $\frac{10}{20} =$ **h.** $\frac{5}{15} =$ **i.** $\frac{16}{18} =$ **j.** $\frac{12}{24} =$ **k.** $\frac{10}{12} =$ **l.** $\frac{8}{12} =$

2.

a. $\frac{6}{18} =$ **b.** $\frac{15}{25} =$ **c.** $\frac{20}{30} =$ **d.** $\frac{50}{100} =$ **e.** $\frac{12}{16} =$ **f.** $\frac{6}{10} =$

g. $\frac{9}{18} =$ **h.** $\frac{4}{8} =$ **i.** $\frac{30}{42} =$ **j.** $\frac{14}{21} =$ **k.** $\frac{9}{27} =$ **l.** $\frac{3}{24} =$

3.

a. $\frac{7}{14} =$ **b.** $\frac{5}{25} =$ **c.** $\frac{6}{30} =$ **d.** $\frac{15}{18} =$ **e.** $\frac{4}{12} =$ **f.** $\frac{8}{16} =$

g. $\frac{10}{40} =$ **h.** $\frac{25}{35} =$ **i.** $\frac{3}{21} =$ **j.** $\frac{6}{24} =$ **k.** $\frac{8}{32} =$ **l.** $\frac{9}{36} =$

Finding a missing term

1.

a. $\frac{5}{8} = \frac{\ }{16}$ **b.** $\frac{2}{3} = \frac{\ }{9}$ **c.** $\frac{1}{5} = \frac{\ }{10}$ **d.** $\frac{2}{4} = \frac{\ }{16}$ **e.** $\frac{4}{5} = \frac{\ }{20}$

f. $\frac{1}{8} = \frac{\ }{24}$ **g.** $\frac{3}{7} = \frac{\ }{14}$ **h.** $\frac{5}{6} = \frac{\ }{12}$ **i.** $\frac{3}{10} = \frac{\ }{30}$ **j.** $\frac{7}{8} = \frac{\ }{48}$

2.

a. $\frac{2}{3} = \frac{10}{\ }$ **b.** $\frac{1}{5} = \frac{4}{\ }$ **c.** $\frac{3}{4} = \frac{15}{\ }$ **d.** $\frac{7}{8} = \frac{21}{\ }$ **e.** $\frac{1}{10} = \frac{3}{\ }$

f. $\frac{5}{7} = \frac{10}{\ }$ **g.** $\frac{9}{10} = \frac{18}{\ }$ **h.** $\frac{4}{11} = \frac{12}{\ }$ **i.** $\frac{7}{15} = \frac{14}{\ }$ **j.** $\frac{3}{5} = \frac{12}{\ }$

3.

a. $\frac{3}{5} = \frac{15}{\ }$ **b.** $\frac{8}{11} = \frac{\ }{22}$ **c.** $\frac{1}{8} = \frac{5}{\ }$ **d.** $\frac{2}{3} = \frac{\ }{18}$ **e.** $\frac{1}{4} = \frac{8}{\ }$

f. $\frac{3}{20} = \frac{6}{\ }$ **g.** $\frac{7}{15} = \frac{28}{\ }$ **h.** $\frac{6}{7} = \frac{\ }{28}$ **i.** $\frac{11}{12} = \frac{33}{\ }$ **j.** $\frac{9}{10} = \frac{\ }{50}$

Renaming of mixed numbers into improper fractions

1.

a. $1\frac{1}{3} = \frac{}{3}$ **b.** $2\frac{1}{4} = \frac{}{4}$ **c.** $2\frac{2}{5} = \frac{}{5}$ **d.** $3\frac{3}{4} = \frac{}{4}$ **e.** $3\frac{2}{3} = \frac{}{3}$

f. $4\frac{1}{5} = \frac{}{5}$ **g.** $3\frac{1}{8} = \frac{}{8}$ **h.** $1\frac{11}{12} = \frac{}{12}$ **i.** $2\frac{6}{7} = \frac{}{7}$ **j.** $5\frac{3}{4} = \frac{}{4}$

2.

a. $3\frac{4}{5} =$ **b.** $2\frac{2}{7} =$ **c.** $1\frac{8}{9} =$ **d.** $4\frac{2}{3} =$ **e.** $6\frac{1}{4} =$

f. $4\frac{3}{4} =$ **g.** $10\frac{1}{3} =$ **h.** $9\frac{1}{6} =$ **i.** $3\frac{5}{6} =$ **j.** $2\frac{10}{11} =$

Renaming of improper fractions into mixed numbers

1.

a. $\frac{10}{3} =$ **b.** $\frac{9}{5} =$ **c.** $\frac{14}{3} =$ **d.** $\frac{12}{5} =$ **e.** $\frac{19}{6} =$ **f.** $\frac{22}{7} =$

g. $\frac{18}{5} =$ **h.** $\frac{15}{4} =$ **i.** $\frac{19}{7} =$ **j.** $\frac{32}{6} =$ **k.** $\frac{81}{10} =$ **l.** $\frac{17}{4} =$

2.

a. $\frac{11}{3} =$ **b.** $\frac{14}{5} =$ **c.** $\frac{18}{7} =$ **d.** $\frac{23}{5} =$ **e.** $\frac{17}{2} =$ **f.** $\frac{63}{8} =$

g. $\frac{17}{3} =$ **h.** $\frac{82}{9} =$ **i.** $\frac{59}{9} =$ **j.** $\frac{32}{7} =$ **k.** $\frac{15}{2} =$ **l.** $\frac{19}{4} =$

Index

276

take-away 17
  with money 35
subtrahend 17
sum 16

T
table form 8-10
terms 111-113
  higher 111-112
  lower 113
time 93-95
time lines 161-163
time zones 165

ton 153
triangle 145

V
volume 222
  comparing 223

W
week 93

Y
yard 148
year 93

Photo Credits

All photographs appearing in **MATH for Christian Schools™**, **Grade 4,** were made by George Collins, except as noted below:

The following paintings were supplied through the courtesy of: